George Overend Drewry, H. Critchett Bartlett

Cup and Platter

Notes on Food and its Effects

George Overend Drewry, H. Critchett Bartlett

Cup and Platter
Notes on Food and its Effects

ISBN/EAN: 9783744645935

Printed in Europe, USA, Canada, Australia, Japan

Cover: Foto ©Andreas Hilbeck / pixelio.de

More available books at **www.hansebooks.com**

CUP AND PLATTER;

OR,

NOTES ON FOOD AND ITS EFFECTS.

BY

G. OVEREND DREWRY, M.D.,

AUTHOR OF "THE COMMON-SENSE MANAGEMENT OF THE STOMACH,"

AND

H. C. BARTLETT, PH.D., F.C.S.

HENRY S. KING & CO., LONDON.
1876.

(The rights of translation and of reproduction are reserved.)

PREFACE.

THESE chapters contain in a condensed form the notes of a series of lectures which were given for the purpose of explaining in a simple manner the most important points in connection with this subject. It is worthy of note that the necessity for action in the matter was felt by the lecturers as the result of their daily observation on the two distinct classes of agents concerned in the processes of digestion and assimilation; namely, those in the body, termed digestive principles, and those outside the body, the various components of food. This was how an analyst whose daily business it is to examine foods, and a physician who devotes himself especially to the treatment of the stomach, from their two distinct fields of observation, were led to the same conclusion. From every logical deduction derived from the most practical experience, it became apparent that a more extended knowledge of this all-important subject must be unfolded to the minds of all classes, both for the successful treatment of diseases, and for the maintenance of health.

Digitized by the Internet Archive
in 2008 with funding from
Microsoft Corporation

http://www.archive.org/details/cupplatterornote00drewrich

CONTENTS.

CHAP.		PAGE
	INTRODUCTION	1
I.	WATER	17
II.	MILK	31
III.	BREADSTUFFS	44
IV.	MEAT, FISH	65, 69
V.	VEGETABLES AND FRUIT	72
VI.	FOOD ACCESSORIES	80
VII.	BEER	86
VIII.	WINE	101
IX.	SPIRITS	117
X.	TEA, COFFEE, COCOA	139
XI.	KITCHEN ILLUSTRATIONS AND COOKERY	147
XII.		156

CUP AND PLATTER:

NOTES ON FOOD AND ITS EFFECTS.

―――•―――

INTRODUCTION.

THE importance of an extended knowledge of the principles which regulate the processes of digestion and assimilation of food cannot be too highly estimated. It is the possession of this knowledge, and this alone, which can enable persons to discriminate between the good and bad in food, to select those foods which are suitable for the purposes required, and to reject those, unfortunately now so common, which are manufactured to secure large profits, altogether without regard to wholesome and judicious composition.

The first great principle which must be realised, is that the body itself, in all its various structures, is composed of different groupings of the same elements as exist in the several kinds of food. The next is, that after the arrangement of the components of food has been altered by the juices with which they come into contact in the body during digestion, by which they are rendered soluble, they are taken up and assimilated, that is, they join the other elements similar to themselves already present in the structure, and in this manner alone new tissue is formed. It is manifest from this that food, to be properly balanced, must contain a sufficiency of all the various components of the body in something like the proportion in which those components are wasted in healthy organisms.

If there is an insufficiency of any of these components, those tissues requiring that particular component necessarily dwindle, being worked off in the splitting up of their composition and the elimination of their waste products, and not having the necessary increment of their own kind to maintain them at their normal standard, they become gradually worn out.

Now, if every one were born healthy, and there were no constitutional diseases, the proper system of diet might soon be arrived at; but inasmuch as, from the earliest times to the present, a certain peculiar tendency to some one particular form of disease, or a deviation from health, has been recognised in each individual, it is of the highest importance to ascertain in which direction the tendency lies. By a well-regulated system of life, and notably by a proper selection of food, we may counteract that disposition, affording in plenty those matters which are lacking, and withholding such as in each individual case tend to form compounds in excess of those necessary for health.

In this way, for example, taking infancy and childhood, the well-known disease called "rickets" is caused by a deficiency of phosphate of lime, on the presence of which solidity of bone depends. A healthy child may be starved into rickets by withholding those components of food, otherwise plentiful, which contain these salts, just as a rickety child may be fed into health by giving food which contains them in full proportion.

In the case of rickets, lime is an absolute necessity; but in the case of children brought up to drink plentifully of water charged with lime, we find Goitre, or Derbyshire neck, all kinds of deposit in the urine, and often stone in the bladder. Here, that which is beneficial to a rickety constitution is most injurious when the system is overcharged. Advancing, we may take the cases of pallor and weakness so common in over-crowded towns and cities, which are due to a want of salts of iron in the blood; in them, the kind of food taken is of the utmost importance, in order that it may provide a sufficiency of such salts.

Again, in constitutional diseases, such as gout, rheumatism, or diabetes, which are well known to depend upon an excessive formation of uric acid, lactic acid, and sugar respectively, the mode of controlling them is obvious, namely, to exclude as much as possible those matters which science teaches us favour the formation of these compounds, and to give those only which will nourish sufficiently without encouraging these diseases.

So, in cases in which there is a difficulty in the absorption and assimilation of various matters, such as fats, which, either in that form or in the form of oil, are incapable of being absorbed, and which require a process similar to that of saponification, it is of the utmost importance, not only to those structures containing them, but to the health of the entire body, that food should contain those matters in that condition, or that the agents necessary to produce it shall be present at the time of digestion.

The converse also holds good in cases where there is a tendency to an excessive deposit of fat, and to a degeneration of the muscular tissues into fat, which is frequently a cause of death. If care be taken to exclude as much as possible those foods which directly tend to form fat, and if a sufficiency of exercise is also insisted upon, this tendency is diminished.

It is, however, of the utmost importance that the

treatment be very gradual, inasmuch as healthy assimilation of the food cannot go on if one component which has been largely taken be suddenly stopped altogether. Such an experiment would be attended with considerable danger.

If, when these postulates have been stated, we regard the nutrition of early infancy, childhood, youth, maturity, and old age, we shall form a correct estimate of the healthy condition of the body under these several periods of life. Natural instinct has not been found wanting in providing food suitable for the sustentation of existence at any stage of the progress of the human body, but science must be regarded as curbing exuberance of appetite or predilection, and on the other hand as producing desire for those foods most suitable when the want of natural vigour has precluded the natural appetite from asserting itself.

At the commencement of human life, milk, and milk only, must be considered the natural food, the milk of the mother, if healthy, being the most desirable of all. In many cases where conditions exist which prevent the child from obtaining a sufficiency of its natural sustenance, the fresh milk of cows, slightly diluted and sweetened, is almost universally found to form a very suitable substitute; but the essential of freshness can never be too strongly insisted upon, as the stomach of a young infant is almost invariably found far too prone to excite acidity in milk foods, whenever the milk itself contains the faintest germs of an acid reaction.

It may be pointed out with the greatest possible emphasis, that milk which is fresh and sweet, as far as taste is concerned, may yet contain the germs that have been alluded to, such conditions being utterly impossible of identification by the adult palate.

From such remarks it may be understood in what manner condensed milk has been found so frequently advantageous as food for infants, and for reasons which are more fully entered into in the consideration of that important item, milk, in its particular classification as food in these chapters. When, however, other food is wanted during infancy, it should never be adopted without medical advice, and particularly without due scrutiny of the character of food recommended.

Starches of all kinds at this period of life must be avoided, and the description of food which is more valuable under these circumstances will be touched upon in due course. As the demands of the body increase both in volume and variety, the amount of starchy matter, such as is exhibited in bread, flour, oatmeal, and vegetables, becomes more admissible, and as progress is made in the digestive functions these are found to be requisites, besides other forms of food which contain more nitrogenous matter, such as meat, fish, eggs, and other strong nourishment of a similar kind.

In gradually leading up to the diet now indicated, we come to the period of youth where all these are necessitated in larger quantities, and when for the first time in this climate a small quantity of light beer or wines of low alcoholicity may be occasionally taken with benefit. In health, perhaps, a greater superstructure of strength may be obtained without the use of any alcoholic fluids; but in many cases the consideration of this question must be left to those most competent to judge whether they are required or not. No pharisaical objection must be taken to good beer or wine, when its use is properly advocated; but until after full maturity of growth this must be generally considered to be but little required.

In adult life the danger to be apprehended from injudicious diet, whether solid or liquid, is certainly at its minimum; but that is only during this particular time. The results of injudicious eating or drinking will be assuredly manifest at a later period, if either of these have been indulged in to any considerable extent. Generous diet is by no means to be despised, especially when bodily exercise carries off any slight superabundance. Meagre diet, on the other hand, is certainly not sufficient to maintain that severe condition of mental exertion or monotony of avocation which are unfortunately the lot of many under the subdivision of labour which now exists.

To remedy the difficulty of digestion and assimilation of strong food in those who are unable to eliminate its waste products, great care should be taken that the nourishment they select should be of such a character as to be easily digestible, and to afford the special nutriment that they require. Fatty matters, which as cerebrin probably carry the phosphatic salts to their destination in the brain and nerves, form important components of the food suitable to persons of sedentary habits of life.

The necessity for this is pointed out in the accompanying diagram which shows the relations of the composition of the various tissues of the body to that of the analysis of the several proximate principles of food. Passing on to that which is demanded by the decline of life, while additional ease of digestibility is a *sine quâ non*, more frequent meals may be consistently advocated, and a more stimulating diet, though less in quantity, is that which experience has found to be most suitable.

Alcoholic fluids, in contradistinction to the more heavily saccharine wines and beers, are frequently found to exert a beneficial influence, and they can be no more dispensed with in many instances than can the nourishing but easily digestible food, just alluded to, as the proper food for persons living under the artificial conditions of civilised life.

The chief ultimate elements forming the proximate principles of food are found in the body as under :—

Elements	Principle	Function in body
Oxygen, Hydrogen	Water,	Of which the body consists to the extent of nearly three-fourths.
Carbon, Hydrogen, Nitrogen, Oxygen	Gelatin,	One of the main components of the cellular and muscular tissues, and particularly of the skin and bones.
Carbon, Hydrogen	Fat,	The adipose tissues and nerve and brain substance.
Carbon, Hydrogen, Oxygen	Starch, gum, and sugar, *In food,*	Are transformed, *In the body,* yielding vital force and sometimes fat.
Phosphorus, Calcium, Oxygen	Phosphate of lime,	The bones, etc.
Carbon, Hydrogen, Nitrogen, Oxygen, Sulphur	Fibrin and Albumin,	The muscular tissues, blood, etc.
Carbon, Calcium, Oxygen	Carbonate of lime,	The bones, etc.

In addition to these—

Chlorine, Sodium, Fluorine, Potassium, Iron, and Magnesium enter into the composition of several of the juices and tissues in different proportions.

In this diagram the identity of the components of food and the constituents of the body are shown, and the mode in which chemical changes occur in organic as in inorganic chemistry may be seen. It may be well to give the shortest possible description of the processes of digestion and assimilation.

The mechanism employed in these processes consists in the organs concerned in mastication, insalivation, deglutition, the action of the stomach, duodenum, lacteals, and absorbents. The reagents which produce the chemical changes in the various kinds of food are contained in the saliva, the gastric fluids, bile, and the pancreatic fluid. The first of these owes its peculiar power of converting starch into sugar to the presence of an albuminoid compound called ptyalin. The solvent power of the gastric juice, which is specially directed to the breaking up of the nitrogenous matters such as meat, consists, again, of another albuminoid fermentative substance termed pepsin, which is only found in activity in conjunction with hydrochloric or other acids; these in themselves are secreted and brought out by the stomach during the process of digestion.

Supposing the digestion of those portions of the food, just alluded to, to have passed so far, the dissolved matter is poured out from the stomach into the duodenum, or upper portion of the intestine, along with the other constituents of the food which have not been acted on by saliva or gastric juice. In this portion of the alimentary canal the mass of food which is called chyme receives the admixture of two most important fluids, the bile and the pancreatic juice.

The action of the bile is a distinctly antiseptic one, preventing the tendency to putrefaction and the development of the gases incident thereto. It also has the vitally important action of the preparation of fatty matters of food for their ultimate solution by the pancreatic fluid.

This is a matter which has been hitherto but little understood; but from some experiments which we have recently made, we have every reason to believe that the essential bearings of the subject will be better understood in the future, and that results will be obtained of such a character as will furnish the clue so long wanting for the successful treatment of those diseases in which emaciation is the most prominent symptom.

The food mass, or chyme, is by this time transformed into a milky fluid called chyle, mixed with those matters which have escaped the action of the process described. Such action continues to a greater or less extent upon these during their passage through the remainder of the intestines; but the cellulose or woody fibre of the vegetables, and the harder or more fibrinous portion of the meat, and a large proportion of starch, still continues its onward progress, and is ultimately disposed of in an undigested form.

The absorption of matters in true solution takes place in the stomach, and these, such as the aqueous portion of soup, saccharine, and alcohol, are taken up by the stomach absorbents. But although this is very rapid with such solutions, the great work of selection and nutrition is accomplished after the food is passed into the intestines. Here, again, is a point, the consideration of which has been much neglected heretofore, viz., the carriers of the chyle, or lacteals, which suck up through the lining membrane of the small intestines, during their entire length, the real nutriment of the food as it passes over them, from thence to be distributed throughout the various tissues of the body; and each of which, in a condition of health, is replenished by a process termed assimilation, or the adding of those matters to themselves which are similar to their composition.

The mode of exemplification adopted at the lectures was very simple, namely, by samples in illustration of the various matters treated upon. Those selected were such as were most worthy of note in regard to their own peculiarities, or as types of the different food values which may in a greater or less degree be found as components of simple or manufactured articles of food.

Some were purchased without the vendors being aware to what purposes they were being applied, some were supplied at the request of the lecturers, in consequence of their properties having been previously ascertained by personal examination, and some found their way to the lecture-hall without any notification from whence they came, or indeed of those who were good enough to send them.

None, however, were submitted as affording any exemplar of the subject touched upon, unless they had, either for the purpose of these lectures, or previously, been subjected to the most rigorous and searching analysis. From this it may be easily understood that many of the samples purchased, supplied, or volunteered, were not considered suitable for exemplification.

It is by no means one of the least pleasing experiences to be able to state emphatically, that in spite of the general disposition to depreciate, we have found to a much larger extent than we anticipated evidences of the attempt to bring forward pure, sound, and unadulterated articles of food, which only require a sufficient guarantee of a uniformity of their quality, and an extended publicity, to enable them to supplant the inferior and sophisticated, if not spurious, articles with which the market is now flooded for the sake of profit.

If we contrast the amount of food deterioration consequent upon ignorance, as compared with that resulting from deliberate dishonesty, there can be but little doubt that want of knowledge is responsible for an incredibly larger proportion of food waste than is due to any villainy of corruption or venality of trade instinct.

Every subject can be divided into as many parts as may be desired; for our present purpose we should wish to save the patience of those interested, and consider, firstly, foods essential, which, to include anything beyond the period of infancy, must comprise water, milk, and breadstuffs. Then, a somewhat discursive selection of the common articles of diet may be found appropriate; after which, a few food accessories, albeit non-essential, are still of too much consequence to be passed over in any general enquiry as to the results produced by the combination of food and food adjuncts commonly taken in the daily diet.

At the present time, scientific opinion is divided as to whether stimulants are to be properly classed as foods or not. In this regard the much larger series of stimulants denominated alcoholic is that alone which is generally alluded to. As yet, the food value of alcoholic fluids is by no means exhaustively determined, and although we incline to the opinion that the important part played by alcoholic fluids in the process of nutrition must be sooner or later generally admitted, still the food value attributed to the so-called non-alcoholic stimulants, tea, coffee, and cocoa, has been frequently over-rated.

Without attributing to each of these articles the power of injury which the ignorant and excessive use of the first two indubitably entails, if from no other point of view than that a larger attention has been devoted to the subject of cocoa in these chapters, it must be recorded in favour of that article, that no evidence at present exists of its having caused nervous irritability, and deterioration of tissue consequent upon that state, which have followed as certainly upon the misuse of tea as upon that of opium or ardent spirits.

One chapter is devoted to the cookery of food. When it is considered that this is neither a matter of economy alone, nor of the gratification of the palate, but, including these, presents the far higher phase of rendering the majority of food either particularly suitable for digestion and assimilation, or of more or less completely spoiling it in all these respects, the space devoted to it cannot be considered too great.

If nature enables us to obtain crude pabulum which merely necessitates selection, ignorance of the real action of heat upon food, as displayed in the rough-and-ready cookery of ordinary life, must be held responsible for the annihilation of at least a large per-centage both of the nutritive value of food, and of its savour.

CHAPTER I.

WATER.

WATER, although it forms a most important constituent of all kinds of food, must here be regarded not as that which is so combined, but such as we obtain from our cisterns and wells, and use either for culinary operations or for more purely drinking purposes.

We are accustomed to note in the newspapers that the water supplied by the great companies is found, upon inspection, to be more or less contaminated, and unfit for consumption.

Some persons suppose that if water were perfectly pure, that is, free from all matters held in solution or suspension, whether animal, vegetable, or mineral, this would be the best adapted for drinking purposes.

Distilled water would fulfil all these requirements, and yet it is almost universally found to be disagreeable, or at least insipid. This arises from the curious fact that distillation of water by ordinary means leaves an almost inappreciable quantity of foreign matter, which is yet sufficient to taint the flavour of the water which has undergone this process. If such precautions be taken as to obviate this almost invariable concomitant, the want of aëration, or the absence of that sparkling quality which is communicated either by carbonic acid gas during the welling up of the purest water from deep chalk springs, or the falling of drops of rain through the air, a certain portion of which is absorbed by them in the passage, they will fully suffice to prove how little desirable the purest waters are for domestic use.

Well aërated rain water has its undoubted value for certain purposes, and at certain periods and conditions of life, particularly with those who are liable to calcic deposits. In this respect it can only be considered valuable for table use in an unmixed form. Externally, for general purposes of ablution, it is certainly advantageous.

For making tea, coffee, and cocoa; brewing, or extracting those soluble matters which perhaps it would accomplish with the greatest economy, it is actually objectionable from its excess of solvent power. The softer waters invariably dissolve out other matters which it is of great importance both in regard to flavour and dietetic excellence to avoid.

Perhaps the finest water obtainable, with which

we are acquainted, is that derived from the previously mentioned deep chalk springs. These contain the smallest possible amount of putrefactive (organic) constituents, and a desirable amount of hardness, so called, from the presence of carbonate of lime or chalk.

When there is an excess of hardness from carbonate of lime, it can only be occasioned by an excess of carbonic acid retained in the water, and this may invariably be removed by the very simple process of boiling. Hardness, however, may be occasioned by other constituents than carbonate of lime. Some of these are objectionable, others directly injurious. Sulphate of lime or gypsum would perhaps be designated as both objectionable and injurious, and large districts are supplied with water containing this salt in considerable quantities.

Various metallic salts of iron, copper, and lead are frequently found in the water supply of many localities, iron existing in a variety of forms soluble in water. The iron-stone formation, or soils in which a certain amount of iron is to be found, invariably furnish salts of iron in waters derived from them, of which chalybeate springs are striking examples.

Waters which tinge all articles of food prepared with them, or stain linen with what is termed iron mould, are familiar enough in many parts of the kingdom; and in these localities the difficulty is to obtain water which is altogether free from this mineral.

The best mode of dealing with this water is by judicious filtration. It demands a very peculiar medium for the removal of this constituent from such waters. The best filters for such purposes are those composed of a particular charcoal, either containing a considerable proportion of carbonate of lime naturally, or in which a large per-centage of this substance has been incorporated.

We have in the course of our enquiries become acquainted with three distinct systems of filtration which accomplish this end. But as these have to be more particularly described with regard to their removal of salts of lead and copper, which are not so much objectionable in flavour and appearance, as really poisonous, we will describe the nature of these salts before proceeding to the explanation of the chemical action of the filters.

The presence of salts of lead, copper, and perhaps some of the rarer metals, in drinking waters, is far more common than is usually supposed. Water that is free from these contaminations nine months in the year may at certain seasons take up and hold with great persistence poisonous quantities of these metals. Without dwelling upon the peculiarities of the waters which naturally contain the mineral constituents of the mining districts, a much greater emphasis must be laid upon the fact that certain other salts, particularly those containing nitric or hydrochloric acids, which are derived from the decomposition of vegetable and animal matters, cause otherwise tolerably pure water to dissolve and hold in solution considerable quantities of many metals with which they may come in contact.

When it is considered that the water supply of Great Britain is chiefly carried in leaden service pipes from the mains, stored in metallic cisterns, and frequently heated in contact with copper, it must become apparent that water in a condition to dissolve any of these metals is accorded every facility for so doing, and there has been less recognition of the evils caused than might have been anticipated. This is undoubtedly due to the fact that the poisonous influence is cumulative, and scarcely discernible in its earlier stages: a certain amount of mischief may exist for a time, and be referred to other causes.

It is only when slow poisoning has proceeded for a considerable time that the effects become so manifest as to demonstrate the cause. Long prior to this, a predisposition to other diseases is noticed, and in the majority of these instances no suspicion attaches to the original causation.

Take lead-poisoning as a type. The most prominent symptoms which reveal themselves in the earlier stages of this condition are usually referred to deranged functions of the liver; these are nervousness, slight numbness of the limbs, chilliness, the various forms of indigestion, especially constipation, and a more or less unhealthy tinge in the skin. It is only when these conditions have advanced to the stage of colic, commonly known as painters' colic, wasting of the limbs, blueness of the nails, and a distinct blue line on the gums, that the true nature of the origin of this train of symptoms is certain to be discovered.

The effect of metallic salts in minute subdivision taken daily is more deadly than the taking of a very much larger quantity of the same poison at intervals can possibly be.

There are chemical as well as physiological reasons for this, inasmuch as the acid salts necessary to cause a considerable amount of solution of lead or other metals are precisely those which accompany the decomposition of vegetable or organic matters; so we find, particularly in the autumn, that the impurities passing into very ordinary sources of drinking water are not only metallic but are those due to the putrefaction of the organic matters. Chlorides, nitrites, and nitrates are usually distinguishable in water at this period of the year, aid analysis determines with great precision the amount of nitrogenous matter.

If this proceeds from previous sewage contaminaton, or indeed from infiltration of organic matters incubative of germ-life, these may produce either the worst forms of zymotic disease, or merely that lowered condition of vitality which predisposes those subjected to it to every form of infection. Were there nothing more specific than the mere putrefaction of vegetable matters liable to taint drinking waters, adequate filtration would be the most available means at present of rendering the water fit to drink; and as these can be combined to a certain extent with other reagents, which are specially adapted for the removal of metallic poisons, great stress may be laid upon the obvious advantages of filtration of water, both by public companies and in the domestic household.

Certain fermentations of organic matters, however, especially those denominated putrefactive, tend undoubtedly to that peculiar diminution of vital force which renders the persons subjected to their influences particularly liable to the action of the specific fever poisons when they are exposed to them. Even with these matters the oxidation occasioned by certain systems of filtration is of the greatest value. Every system of filtration fails in the removal of the specific poison germs conveyed by any means, excretal or otherwise, into drinking waters; hence the necessity for obtaining water for table use from the purest possible sources.

Undoubtedly, water obtained from deep chalk springs may have been originally tainted with every kind of impurity, including germs of the worst specific poisons; but in the slow filtration and oxidation incident upon passing through many hundred feet of the least pervious chalk formations, the excessive length of time, or chemical action so produced, is alone found equal to the perfect purification of surface waters.

The estimate formed by certain engineers as to the period requisite for surface water to find its way into the lower stratification from which it is obtained in these springs is so extraordinary, that we can only allude to the suggestion as manifestly absurd. It is, however, certain that no filtration through a sufficient depth of this filtering medium can be accomplished artificially. For this, and for many other reasons scarcely within the province of these pages, it is impossible to discuss the vast system of filtration necessary or advisable on the part of the water companies, inasmuch as it is scarcely probable that a company will ever be able to deal with water derived from rivers in such a manner as to render them either safe or altogether agreeable, particularly, as long as vast quantities of sewage are permitted to flow into our water supplies above the reservoirs.

It becomes the more incumbent upon us to provide ourselves with the best means of obviating those conditions which are so frequently reported in the *Times* or other papers. Turbidity of water, and its containing living organisms and fungoid growths, to say nothing of the fishes and worms often found in domestic cisterns, are evidences vouched for by the officials appointed by Government to inspect the water supply of this metropolis, and our own investigations prove an impregnation with matters far worse than any of these.

The construction of those filters which we have found most suitable for the removal of organic matters has uniformly been that in which means are adopted to prevent any great pressure of the water through the medium. In one of the Silicated Carbon filters this is admirably accomplished by making the only porous surface of the first chamber into which the water flows one of its upright walls. This prevents the formation of a sediment on the top of the usual flat diaphragm when the water comes in contact with this as a second filtering bed.

In another filter, that of Mr. Rawlings, a somewhat similar action is obtained by the admission of the water in such a way that it is distributed from a cup-shaped vessel over the surface of the filtering medium, the effect being in both instances a tendency to prevent the accumulation of deposit from mere gravitation.

The only media we have found of any real value in the oxidation of organic matters, and as secondarily available for the removal of precipitated lead from water, are the charcoals, either animal or mineral; those formed from wood or other vegetable sources being much less efficient.

In treating of filters, one of the most important matters to be invariably borne in mind is, that no matter how valuable the filtering medium may be, it can only remain effective for a certain period of time. Of course the length of time a filter will remain effective depends on the amount of matter to be removed from water, the quantity of water passing through the filter daily, and the frequency with which the upper chamber of the filter is cleansed; but the purifying action of the charcoal must sooner or later come to an end. According to our experience this occurs much more rapidly than is generally stated.

Far greater confidence might be placed upon a system of domestic filtration if filter makers would warn their customers that the filtering medium will have to be removed periodically; and if we say that with the inferior waters, such as those supplied

Water. 27

by certain water companies, no domestic filter supplying an ordinary-sized house can be considered to do its work efficiently for more than twelve months, we shall be according a far greater continuance of filtering power than is possessed by any but the best.

With a better class of water perhaps such filter may last twice as long, but it may be laid down as an axiom that no filter can be relied on for more than twelve months without renewal of the filtering medium.

Considerable attention has been arrested by certain disclosures lately made with regard to the impurities and poisonous properties of a large section of the mineral waters now manufactured. From a very exhaustive examination of these, specially undertaken to determine the amount of these contaminations, we have been greatly struck both with the organic impurities of waters used, and the metallic poisons introduced by the present abominable method of manufacture, in the coarse mechanical endeavour to imitate the natural effervescent springs.

The common aërated water makers have been content to impregnate inferior water with crude carbonic acid, which carbonic acid is generated or retained in lead-lined vessels. When it is considered that water containing an excess of carbonic acid, which is the only cause of the effervescence of these waters, both dissolves and holds in solution large quantities of lead, it must be seen that the receivers and pipes afford the metal for this poisonous solution to the greatest possible extent; and as some of these are jointed and brought into immediate contact with copper and brass fittings, the rapidity of this solution is greatly accelerated by the galvanic action which is necessarily produced.

To demonstrate this impregnation of aërated waters with lead we had only to send out and procure some of the lemonade and soda water extensively sold in the neighbourhood to show a powerful reaction with sulphuretted hydrogen, blackening the water, and even rendering it turbid: from a grain to a grain and a half of lead to the gallon was reached in some of the samples examined. We are glad to say that in those instances where proper precautions had been taken to exclude lead from contact with aërated water, the waters so produced were found free from all trace of this poison, but in almost all samples of lemonade certain small quantities of lead were detected, evidently introduced during the process of concentration of citric acid in leaden vessels.

For this reason several of the German effervescent mineral waters have deservedly borne a high reputation. Bottled at the natural springs, free from metallic and organic impurity, selzer water from Nassau, Apollinaris and other waters, may be said to be absolutely pure from organic or metallic pollutions; the saline ingredients of selzer water, however, contain by far too large a proportion of chloride of sodium (common salt) to render it particularly suitable for assuaging thirst, and it is therefore the less to be advocated as an ordinary beverage.

On account of the large constituent of mineral matters to be found in many of these German waters, they are, according to the salts they contain, particularly efficacious in the treatment of many constitutional disorders. This efficacy has been so long well attested, that it is unnecessary to enlarge upon their medicinal effects; we wish, however, to point out that they are not as perfect in their combinations as is desirable, from the fact that they are almost all imbued with accidental ingredients which diminish their curative value, as well as render them nauseous. We do not see how these adventitious constituents can be eliminated from the natural waters; some, for instance, such as sulphuretted hydrogen and other sulphur compounds, must always militate against the general use of these otherwise valuable waters. Efforts are now being made to reproduce the most desirable of these free from accidental objectionable constituents, both in the form of a pure aërated liquid and in the shape of a concrete substance. Our experience of the effect produced by these purified salines has been highly favourable in comparison with those obtained direct from the natural springs.

CHAPTER II.

MILK.

MILK is correctly stated to be the only food complete in itself. Not only is milk furnished with every requisite of nutrition, but for a certain period of life, that of early infancy, it is the only food required in a condition of health, and in many instances the addition of any other description of food besides milk is absolutely injurious.

The natural secretion which is provided for all young animals, varying only in the proportion of its constituents, is curiously enough adapted to the necessities of the younger carnivora whose future diet is flesh alone, and for the little lambs who will ultimately browse upon herbage. Milk is therefore the universal food, as well as the perfect food, for the whole range of mammalia.

It must not be supposed that milk contains, either in the principles of its composition, or in their relative proportions, the strong meat fit for the sustentation of mature life.

The great divergence before alluded to, between

flesh on the one hand and vegetable food on the other, is quite sufficient to prove that milk by itself cannot replace the diet suited to the instincts of animal life after the earlier portion of its existence. If this be granted with regard to the carnivora and herbivora, the analogy will hold good when the natural instincts predispose to an omnivorous diet, whether these be exhibited among four-footed mammals or by human bipeds. It is therefore necessary to clear away the oft-repeated error that the milk diet, however essential in infancy, is a proper and judicious food to place entire dependence on in after life.

Regarding milk in its very essence as a food, it must be taken from the standpoint of its use as nourishment from the moment of birth. When the first natural secretion of milk is obtained, whether from the human mother or the cow, it is composed of ingredients very different in proportion and quality from that of the milk intended for the subsistence of the young animal. Its first peculiarity is that it contains a large excess of solid matters generally, and particularly an excess of mineral matters or salts, which cause it to assume a purgative action.

The first milk of the cow is termed beastings by the dairymen, and its extra richness and yellow colour is sometimes shown in the milk retailed by them. It cannot, however, be considered advisable to distribute this mixed up with the later milk of other cows. In the human subject the peculiarity of the first milk is of a like nature, and is termed colostrum.

Human milk contains about eleven per cent. of solids, in which the sugar greatly preponderates. Neither the casein or cheesy matter nor the butter is nearly so abundant as in the milk of the cow; nor are the salts contained in the human milk present to the extent of much more than a third of those found in cows' milk. From this it is evident that in all attempts to feed infants upon cows' milk, it must be reduced by the addition of water to such an extent as will somewhat approximate it to the milk derivable from a healthy natural source.

This may be roughly stated to be accomplished by the addition of one-third water, and a little sugar. The reason for this dilution of cows' milk when employed for infant feeding will be better shown by contrasting the amount of solids and their composition; and to render this comparison more complete it may be as well to subjoin particulars of the components of the milk of asses and goats. Both of these have been frequently prescribed and used as substitutes for human milk when cows' milk has been found to disagree. The milk of the cow averages about thirteen to fourteen per cent. of solids, of which the casein forms about one-third part. This, however, varies to some extent inversely with the amount of butter present. The quantity of sugar of milk is perhaps more constant, but in all really good dairy milk the amount of salts, composed of phosphoric acid, lime, and magnesia, almost invariably reaches as much as seven parts in a thousand. The solids of asses' milk more nearly approximate to those of the human mother, being about ten per cent. Of these the cheesy matters and butter bear but a small proportion, while the sugar is present to the extent of about half the total solids. The salts or mineral matters are about half those in cows' milk, and therefore more nearly resemble the human secretion in this respect. Goats' milk, on the other hand, bears a closer similarity to that of cows, the casein or cheesy matter predominating in this instance; and goats' milk can only be considered as more closely approaching the natural food of the infant inasmuch as there is less butter, and considerably less salts.

In alluding to the difference of proportion in the composition of different milks, a much greater attention might have been accorded to the amount, small as it is, of albumin, or the equivalent of the white of egg, which is to be found in milk of all kinds.

The albumin present is at first in a highly soluble form, and is therefore particularly easy of digestion in that condition. It is, however, very prone to decomposition, and not only to decompose of itself, but also to excite fermentation in the other constituents of the milk. To such an extent is this the case, that in warm weather a distinct change can be detected within a few hours of milking, if the milk has not been rapidly and efficiently cooled directly it is obtained.

When examined under the microscope, milk which has been carelessly treated or allowed to retain too high a temperature, commences to exhibit the peculiar germs of lactous fermentation. These germs are distinct evidence of an acid change long before any acidity can be detected by the palate; and among other reasons for the early development of this very undesirable fermentation, one must be particularly alluded to. Any neglect of the most scrupulous cleanliness in the milking sheds, or vessels into which the milk is drawn, or in the coolers or cans, or any other utensils with which the milk may come in contact, or even a close or unhealthy atmosphere, may prove sufficient not only to set up this process of lactous fermentation, but as the milk is highly absorbent of the minutest particles which are carried by air, bad flavour may be communicated, and noxious influences disseminated, unless the most careful precautions are observed to prevent the possibility of contamination.

The influence of the surrounding air upon milk is greatly increased when the large bulk collected in churns after cooling is again divided into small quantities, and as in all instances the smaller the quantities of liquid so exposed, the greater the amount of surface subjected to the aëreal or gaseous influences, so the advantage of systematically closing and sealing up all the small cans used in distributing milk is quite evident, irrespective of the security it affords against adulteration with water, or the abstraction of the cream. In other words, most of the contamination and all adulteration generally believed to take place somehow between the dairy farm and the consumer is prevented by means at once simple, satisfactory, and inexpensive.

We believe that this method was first adopted by the Aylesbury Dairy Company, as a valuable safeguard in addition to their other means for preventing sophistication or any possible contamination.

However good the general average of milk in any given district may be, it must always be borne in mind that the character and flavour must vary considerably according to the season of the year and the mode of feeding adopted. In summer, when the cows can roam among pastures and obtain a plentiful supply of rich, juicy, and suitable grazing, it is well known that the quality of the milk and its peculiarly characteristic odour are greatly enhanced, and it is at this period that the finest-flavoured butter is alone procurable.

When in the winter months cows are stall fed, and in addition to hay, turnips, oil-cake, and other artificial foods form a large proportion of their daily diet, the strong flavours introduced thereby into the milk and butter derived from it are peculiarly obnoxious to many persons of delicate taste. This is a sufficient reason for the repugnance frequently evinced by infants for cows' milk under these conditions.

It is also unfortunate that a very much larger quantity of milk is obtainable in summer than in winter, the drawback being that in many districts it is altogether impossible to convey it to market while still sufficiently fresh for feeding infants. The well-known effects produced upon many persons by eating turnips, carrots, etc., are strangely enough reproducible on partaking of the milk supplied from cows fed upon these root crops.

Great inconvenience frequently arises from the flatulent distention occasioned from this source: this is a fact well known to every mother of a family, and we cannot devote too great attention to the feeding of our milch cattle to prevent the ill effects so constantly produced from these and other causes.

A great step has been made towards equalising the supply of milk at all seasons of the year by condensing it. When milk is cheapest and best, it is produced in the largest quantities, and is most likely to turn sour. The large milk-condensing establishments can then obtain the richest milk, and treat it so as to afford the best summer milkings, which, by the simple addition of water, can be reproduced in the most convenient form at a time when such milk is not otherwise obtainable.

A great prejudice existed at first against condensed milk. This was no doubt originally occasioned by the idea that that forwarded from Switzerland was composed principally of goats' milk. This was not the case, as its analysis conclusively proved. A slight difference of flavour tended to augment this prejudice, and it was not evident, until the late Dr. Edward Smith attempted to show that the milk itself was really inferior, that the attention of those qualified to judge was directed to it for the purpose of setting the question at rest. Unfounded opposition has frequently been the means of bringing out the proper merits of many scientific improvements in the preparation of food, but never, perhaps, with greater *éclat* than in this instance.

Analyses were made of the condensed milks, proving them to be very superior to most of the milk sold prior to the passing of the adulteration of food act. The effects of using this condensed milk were watched attentively by the medical profession, and the result now is that condensed milk is almost universally recommended as the best source of obtaining really wholesome milk in a condition of greater uniformity than can be obtained from any of the smaller dairies.

The sugar which is necessary to maintain the semi-fluidity of condensed milk is by no means objectionable. For infants' food, as we have pointed out, a certain amount of sugar must be added to the diluted cow's milk before it becomes a suitable substitute for the milk of the mother; in fact, the only drawback incident to condensed milk is the slight peculiarity of flavour which it communicates to tea or delicate puddings, custards, etc.

No greater mistake could have been made in the estimation of the value of milk than that resulting from the crude and misleading mode generally adopted. In the first place, the glass instrument termed by the sellers a lactometer is roughly adjusted to show by the specific gravity of the milk to what extent it is supposed to be watered. We have seen an instrument of this kind, the stem of which was divided into four parts, marked pure milk, quarter water, half water, three-quarters water, and all water. These are still sold for about 1s. 6d., and have been largely purchased under the delusion that they would afford some indication of the quality of the milk.

Now, if we consider that the fatty matters are much lighter than water, and that the cheesy matters are much heavier than water, and that the proportion of water varies in perfectly pure milk to some extent, it must be evident, at once, that as the butter and cheesy matters are greater or less, so the specific gravity of the milk must be proportionably higher or lower in milk to which no water has been added; in fact, the highest specific gravity would be shown by a milk from which the greater part of the cream had been abstracted.

Fraudulent milk-dealers were well acquainted with this fact, and, taking advantage of it, first skimmed off the cream, and then lowered the specific gravity by means of the addition of water, producing that indication in the lactometer which exactly accorded with pure milk.

Some progress has been made in the detection

Milk. 41

of adulteration in milk; but even now, at the hands of many so-called analysts, the false assumption is made that the mere proportion of water capable of being dried out of a given sample of milk will furnish accurate indications from which the amount of admixture of water with the milk can be ascertained. The truth is, that the examination of milk to ascertain its purity and suitability as food for delicate infants and invalids is one necessitating a far more elaborate system of analysis than can possibly be accorded for any of the fees which are own paid for making it.

If it is considered worth while to pay fees of from three to ten guineas for accurate and complete quantitative analyses of milk for the great dairy companies and the condensed milk factories, so that they may obtain reliable data on which to conduct their operations, no one will be surprised to find the most absurd discrepancies of result in the perfunctory analyses now so commonly put forward.

Perhaps, scarcely sufficient emphasis has been laid upon the immediate use, for the purpose of feeding children, of milk which has been recently obtained; and at the risk of seeming to repeat the caution against the use of milk in which fermentation has commenced, we wish to draw particular attention to the fact that the spores or cells which are found in the mouths of children suffering from that condition, commonly known as thrush, are identical with those in milk fungus, which ultimately form blue mould on the surface of milk long exposed to the air. The smallest particle of milk fungus is sufficient to cause germination of growths throughout the newest and freshest milk.

Here, we have the direct cause of thrush in infants from carelessness in cleansing the vessels in which the milk is kept, and the feeding bottles in which it is conveyed to the child; and as a hint which will be found valuable in the administration of milk by the feeding bottle, it may be as well to remark that there is a want of sufficient attention to the very important fact that the natural temperature of milk from the breast is invariably that of the blood, namely, about 100° Fahrenheit, and milk and water for feeding should be therefore maintained as nearly as possible at this temperature. This can only be ascertained by means of the thermometer.

In adult life there are many diseases in which the use of milk as a principal article of diet is strongly indicated, and in others as much to be avoided; and it is only upon close investigation of the conditions of the body, and its digestive organs, that satisfactory conclusions can be arrived at; but, generally speaking, it must be considered one of the great reasons why a milk diet has been in many cases tried and discarded as valueless, that many other articles of food have been taken at the same time which are not compatible with it. The result in this instance is the formation of large masses of curd and cheese, so to speak, which are necessarily productive of the most objectionable results. On the other hand, the value of a well-regulated milk diet, in conjunction with other suitable foods, cannot be over-estimated in cases where, from long previous mismanagement, the digestive powers have become impaired. In these, as in infancy, all the elements of nutrition are thus presented in a condition requiring the smallest digestive effort, and rest for the digestive organs is obtained, whilst the nutrition of the body is adequately accomplished.

CHAPTER III.

BREADSTUFFS.

TWENTY years ago, when the microscope was first brought to bear upon the examination of the breadstuffs in common use, the immediate result of its revelations was a general scare. The popular notion of bread, at least in England, presupposed that made of only one kind of cereal, in the form of very finely dressed flour.

If the most overweening confidence was placed in the staff of life, a term of which bread seems to have enjoyed a monopoly, that confidence was shaken to its very foundation by a statement to the effect that the flour of barley, oats, beans, peas, rice, and many other grains had been detected in ordinary bakers' bread; and not only so, but that many other matters not coming properly within the definition of breadstuffs, such as sulphate of copper, alum, and plaster of Paris, together with other mineral abominations under the term of "Jonathan," besides a heavy leavening with mashed potatoes, were proved to be used by bakers.

At this period by far the larger quantity of bread in common use was that termed households, and was made, or supposed to have been made, of that description of white flour bearing the same name. An inferior description of bread was also sold, made of what is known as seconds flour, and bearing the same designation. The more expensive kind was sold either as best or fancy bread. In addition to these, brown bread, milk loaves, French and tinned loaves, were all of them in much more moderate demand; but the real old-fashioned bread of the past century could hardly be purchased throughout the length and breadth of the land.

In Scotland, oat cakes, pease bannocks, bean and pea bread, rye cakes, are now gradually being exchanged for the ordinary whiter breads familiar to English consumers. But on the Continent the great mass of the breadstuffs forming that portion of the food of the people is still of a more varied and coarser description.

Between all those varieties, which, if space would permit, might include many others, it may be of some little service to point out wherein consists the true nutritive value in a greater or less proportion of the various cereals. From the following table, the average components of the meals and flours which are in common use can be compared:—

TABLE

Of average components of Meals and Flours in common use :—

	Wheat.	Wheaten Flour.	Barley.	Oatmeal.	Maize.	Peas.	Beans.	Rice.	Potatoes.
Water ...	14·1	15·0	15·9	15·5	13·7	14·3	10·1	10·0	72·1
Nitrogenous matter ..	13·4	10·8	7·3	12·3	8·1	22·1	24·5	5·1	1·7
Starch, gum, sugar, etc.	67·7	70·5	72·3	64·2	69·9	58·9	59·2	83·6	25·1
Fat.....	2·1	2·0	2·4	5·2	6·9	2·1	2·9	·7	·3
Mineral matter	2·7	1·7	2·1	2·8	1·4	2·6	3·3	·6	·8

As far as their composition is concerned, it will not be difficult to comprehend the separate and distinct uses to which they may at different times be applied. Wheat undoubtedly occupies the first place in the estimation of Englishmen. Wheaten bread may now be found forming the most substantial portion of the daily food in this country. As such, every portion of the grain must be regarded according to the quantity and digestibility of the nourishment it affords. But as certain portions produce immediate effects other than those of mere nutrition, it will be necessary to particularise as briefly as possible the peculiarities of each.

When wheat is well grown and soundly harvested, it soon attains that condition which fits it for being made into bread of several kinds, the most ancient method being to subject the grain to a heavy pounding in a rude mortar of wood or stone. The exterior portion of the husk, which becomes easily detached during this process, was simply winnowed away by blowing with the mouth, and with these latter particulars we have nothing to do.

The heavier cortex or covering of the grain itself is of a somewhat complicated structure. No less than five separate cuticles or skins have been shown to exist. Within the cellular formation of these skins a curious fermentative albuminous principle is found, which in itself not only affords a most valuable nutritive quality, but has also the effect of rendering the flour of the kernel more easy of conversion into a digestible condition, and materially assists in a rude panification or bread-making, which, however primitive, affords a strong and healthy food staple.

This process of making bread from wheat, as adopted in more ancient times, is still practised in many eastern countries; and, as if to show an inevitable cycle in the annals of food, as of other historical events, more recent researches into the food value of various descriptions of bread are now tending towards the re-establishment in public favour of whole meal bread not altogether dissimilar to that made by the rough-and-ready process just described.

Prior to the efforts which have been made within the last few years to show the nature and proportions of the nourishment to be found in the different portions of the grain, the fashion for extremely white bread had been almost universally accepted. From the finest wheat bread—prepared by the most costly methods of selection, ground by the most exquisite machinery into the finest and most impalpable of flours, dressed through silken sieves, until only that portion which would yield a bread of the most dazzling whiteness was retained—to the commoner and cheaper bread upon which the poorer classes have so much to depend, the desire for whiteness and whiteness alone was the one test which was applied to both the flour and the bread.

Unfortunately, great beauty of colour is not compatible with any mixture of the outer covering of the grain; and, as in the outer portion both of the kernel and covering the larger proportion of nitrogenous, fatty, and mineral matters is contained, bread with an undue preponderance of starch has been that which has met with the greatest favour and demand. No scientific writer upon the subject would object to the utilisation of all the starchy matters contained in wheat flour. But we are of opinion that, for the general nourishment of the people, it is both wasteful and injurious that the mere starchy portion of the wheat should be used, to the exclusion of those other portions which contain the largest proportion of muscle, bone, and other tissue-formers, and which, indeed, confer upon wheat its manifest superiority over any other kind of grain as a combination of nutriment.

No bread, properly so called, can be made from any other grains than those of wheat and barley by themselves. If flour made from any other grain is attempted to be raised into spongy or vesiculated bread, a satisfactory result cannot be obtained. This arises from the want of the gluten in all other kinds of flour. A certain quantity of any of the other flours may, however, be mixed with wheat flour, which will enable it to take the form desired. It is for this reason, doubtless, that wherever fermented bread is required to be made, wheat has always been considered the most valuable of breadstuffs, holding, as it does, a high position in the nutritive scale, as regards the amount of gluten, nitrogenous, and flesh-forming principle.

The injury and fraud which is occasioned by the

introduction of any considerable quantity of potato or rice flour must become at once evident, inasmuch as these tend only to increase the proportion of starch in the bread, and destroy that balance of the various principles which have been found to be so admirably formed by nature in wheat flour. If any great economy could be shown in the use of rice or potatoes for this purpose, their weakness in this regard should be counteracted by the addition of some of the more nitrogenous flours. For this purpose oatmeal, pea and bean flour, and, perhaps, the flour of some other grain, now little known in England, but extensively used in India, might be judiciously employed; always bearing in mind that all these possess strong flavours disagreeable to many, and are, besides, undoubtedly difficult of digestion, and of a consistence which can only be obviated by a method of cooking especially adapted for them. Long simmering at a temperature of about 180° renders peas, beans, lentils, and other leguminous seeds fit to be used as food, and without this they ought not to be introduced into bread which is only subjected to a brief period of ordinary baking.

The general means adopted in the manufacture of bread, to render it light and spongy, is that occasioned by the fermentative action of yeast upon the dough, the chemical effect of which is to evolve carbonic acid gas, steam, and a certain small quantity of vapour of alcohol, by the splitting up of the constituents sugar and starch into these compounds. If there were no true gluten, which is a viscid substance somewhat similar to birdlime, the gaseous matters would at once force their way through the dough, and disappear; but when there is a due proportion of gluten in the dough, its tenacity enables the little puffs, or bubbles of gas, to be imprisoned in the mass which now takes the form technically termed sponge. The art of the baker consists in being able so to regulate the evolution of gas, that it shall neither be formed so rapidly as to force its way through, notwithstanding the gluten, nor so slowly and irregularly as to leave any portion of the bread solid.

Everything depends upon the condition of the flour, the relative proportions of gluten and starchy matters contained in it, and the experience or ability with which the dough is worked up with the yeast. The difference observed in bread baked under the most advantageous circumstances, as compared with bread carelessly prepared, or neglected at any stage, is the difference between bread that is both wholesome and pleasant, and bread which can be neither one nor the other.

Objection has been taken to the impurities introduced in common bakers' yeast. These are, in themselves, undoubtedly, a source of much of the sourness and bad flavour with which we are familiar in bread, and we can confidently assert that if the general public were aware of the putrid condition and disgusting effluvia, to say nothing of the fungoid and other growths induced thereby, attention would be demanded on the part of the inspectors, under the Adulteration Act, to put a stop to the use of ferments in various stages of decomposition.

The whole subject of bread-making, as carried out in the ordinary bakers' cellars, is one so teeming with all that is repulsive, that even adequate description is impossible in all its loathsome details. The personal habits of the poor men, who have to work at the most unseasonable of hours, and continue their exertions throughout so large a portion of the day and night, are almost necessarily opposed to all our ideas of cleanliness and decency. Frequently sleeping in the bakehouse before kneading the dough, they proceed with violent exertion to accomplish this laborious process whilst a considerable portion of their naked bodies streams with perspiration, as they dash their arms beyond the elbows into the viscid mass.

The accommodation provided for ablution prior to engaging in their heavy labour is seldom such as would meet the approval of the least fastidious.

We are afraid that very few of the master bakers make such a personal inspection of their men as can enable them to declare truthfully that they are in any respect fit to be employed upon an operation which demands such scrupulous cleanliness. In touching as lightly as possible upon the filth incident to the common operation of bread-making thus carried out, we have no wish to assume that there are no exceptions to this deplorable state of things; on the contrary, we have ourselves inspected several large bakeries, where the attention to cleanliness in this particular leaves nothing to be desired.* Three methods have come before our notice by which the risk of contamination from bad yeast and personal contact is most efficiently guarded against. The first is that in which the use of yeast is altogether superseded by the production of carbonic acid gas, resulting from the admixture of hydrochloric acid with pure bicarbonate of soda in the bread; the effect of this is to leave in it a small proportion of chloride of sodium (common salt). So small is the proportion left in the bread, when this is properly carried out, that some additional salt has always to be added to the bread to give it the requisite flavour. There can, therefore, be no objection whatever to such a

* Notably, the cleanliness of Perkin's steam bakeries, as worked by Messrs. Hill and Son.

plan when the soda and acid are of ascertained purity.

The second plan has been very successfully worked on a large scale by first generating carbonic acid in a separate vessel, at a great pressure, and then regulating its admixture with the dough by an admirable mechanical contrivance. In addition to this safeguard, machinery has been adapted to the kneading of the dough in close vessels. Without going into the mechanical details, sacks of flour are emptied into a hopper at the top of the building, the flour is mixed with the proper quantity of water, the dough thus made is impregnated with carbonic acid, and at the bottom of the receptacle where this operation takes place there is an opening from whence the dough as fit for baking is expelled and cut off, falling into tins, which are then immediately placed in the oven, the bread never having come in contact with any portion of the baker's person.*

We have thus described two different means of obviating the necessity of using yeast if desired, and also proved by personal investigation that mechanical kneading of the dough will produce bread in every respect as light and as perfect as can be obtained by manual labour. In our objection to the use of yeast when acid or decomposed,

* Bread made by this process is called aërated bread.

we have laid much stress upon the evils which result from it in that condition, but again we should wish to be understood that there is no necessity for the employment of unsound yeast, inasmuch as yeast is capable of being delivered at a considerable distance before any such decomposition can possibly occur. In proof of this we have had samples forwarded from Austria, France, and Holland, which, to our surprise, proved far purer than the generality of brewers' yeast in this country. Under the microscope, the cells were seen to be perfectly clean, well developed, and full of germinating nuclei plainly ready to burst forth into the most vigorous life, when subjected to a suitable temperature after mixing with the flour and water.

The importance of ascertaining the purity of yeast is one which seems to have been greatly underrated, and we are convinced that if personal cleanliness on the part of the baker's journeyman were insisted on, or the mechanical arrangements which have been described were generally adopted, we should require nothing more as a guarantee than the soundness of the condition of the flour, and the absence of false ferments or decomposition in the yeast, to provide bread infinitely more nourishing, wholesome, and agreeable, than that usually found even in shops of considerable pretensions.

From the foregoing tables it will be seen that starch forms by far the largest proportion of the nutritious principles comprised in breadstuffs; and including the potato with these we have represented the compounds of starch with other food principles which are of such vital importance to the nutrition of the body.

It is necessary, here, to describe the use of starch, and the changes which it has to undergo when taken into the body, before it can be assimilated or absorbed. Starch is composed of carbon, oxygen, and hydrogen. There can be little doubt that the largest amount of carbon necessary to the body is introduced by the splitting up of the elements of the starch. Oxygen is also liberated, and performs its most important functions in the internal economy. But before starch can be dissolved and so absorbed, it is necessary that it shall be converted into a soluble form by the action of a vegetable or animal ferment.

Practically, we take starch, after its conversion by vegetable ferments, in the shape of sugar; and it is equally essential, when unchanged starch is eaten, that the animal fermentative principle contained in the saliva, called ptyalin, shall be intimately blended with the starchy food during its mastication in the mouth, so that in its passage through the stomach, and chiefly in its second passage through the intestines, it may become similarly converted into sugar, which, being completely soluble, is taken up by the absorbents. A certain portion of the starchy matter is also converted by the pancreatic juice, also a nitrogenous ferment, the action of which is chiefly directed to fatty matters. But it must be emphatically pointed out that unless this conversion of starch does take place, it cannot be absorbed or assimilated. It must either pass out of the body unchanged, or decompose by putrefaction.

The lactous fermentation which occurs gives rise to unhealthy conditions, and it is only when the starch has been properly converted into sugar, or absorbed, that its constituent carbon, oxygen, and hydrogen are gradually separated, and form the compounds which are finally excreted in the form of carbonates, carbonic acid, and ammonia. If these changes are impeded or arrested, an excess of uric or it may be lactic acid is formed in the system, constituting the material of disease in gout and rheumatism; hence the necessity for taking starch in such moderation that it can be acted upon by the amount of saliva available for its solution: and considerable stress must be laid upon the extreme value of its thorough mastication.

For this reason, as is well known, stale bread is more wholesome than new. The mastication it demands before it can be swallowed is sufficient to ensure proper admixture with the saliva, whereas with a softer and more easily swallowed crumb of new bread, many persons have not appreciated the necessity of retaining it in the mouth long enough for this admixture to take place.

In one of the most intractable of diseases, namely, diabetes, which depends upon the excessive formation of sugar in the body, the most obvious mode that we have of controlling the disease is to reduce the supply of starchy matter. For this purpose a bread is made from which almost the whole of the starch has been removed, and which therefore consists mainly of nitrogenous and mineral matter; but the entire withholding of starchy matters, so frequently insisted on in the treatment of this disease, cannot be said to be warranted by results. We are strongly of opinion that unless a certain portion of starch and sugar be permitted, the assimilation of the other nutritious principles of food generally cannot be satisfactorily carried out.

If our attempt has been successful in showing that the most complete nutrition derivable from wheat is only to be obtained when the whole of the grain is bruised without separating any of the flour from the different portions of the external envelope, it must be obvious that when such bruised grain is made into bread, the entire nutritive value is secured. Certain difficulties stand in the way of accomplishing this, and it is not to every baker that it is given to strike so far aside from his ordinary handicraft as to be able to accomplish the baking of a tolerable loaf of bread from such materials.

In the first place, it is unfortunately not easy to procure whole meal of the requisite quality.

The difficulties of dealing with the preparation of such meal are incident to the general use of mill stones instead of the primitive pestle and mortar. No doubt, ordinary malt rollers would accomplish every object, but we fear few mills supplying bakers are possessed of these very useful contrivances. Whole meal from wheat is, however, to be obtained, and as the matter has already been scientifically considered, very little has been left to be accomplished in the mode of preparation of this meal by those few millers who have already established a reputation for its production. In the same way very few baking firms have encountered the difficulties to be overcome in making palatable bread from the best whole meal.

Here, again, the impediments due to the mechanical details of ordinary bread-making, and those obstacles which invariably intrude themselves where any rule-of-thumb practice is depended upon, have been most successfully surmounted by the indomitable perseverance of one or two more enlightened purveyors, and we have great pleasure in testifying to their success. In dealing with this certainly refractory material for bread-making, altogether beside the question of deriving the full nutritive profit which is obtainable from wheat, there are other considerations of the very greatest moment immediately connected with the use, occasional or habitual, of whole meal bread, which, be it understood, is something considerably different, and very superior in its effectiveness, from the ordinary brown bread, sometimes recommended, but which frequently falls far short of the effect which it is intended to produce.

The essential difference between common brown bread and the whole meal bread of which we have spoken, is that brown bread consists of ordinary flour with a certain amount of ground bran re-mixed with it; but the latter ought never to be ground at all, as it contains the invaluable cerealin and certain other portions of the envelope, and the outer cortex should not be broken into spiculæ, or sharp-pointed fragments, but merely bruised. In this form the immediate action upon the bowels is rather stimulative than irritant, inasmuch as the peristaltic or vermicular movement is accelerated by the passage of those harder portions, and is not to any considerable extent scratched or irritated by any undue breaking up into angular fragments. In addition to this there is an absence of those thin scales into which bran is ordinarily rubbed, which remain as sources of irritation.

Dealing with breadstuffs in their application to bread alone, we have endeavoured to put forward points of most general interest, and at the same time of the highest importance. But in addition to these, a very large amount of the same flours and meals have to be considered in their relations to other foods under the generic term "Farinaceous." It would be useless to recapitulate what has been already stated with regard to the constituents of these substances, but it becomes a still greater necessity at this time when so many absurd doctrines are promulgated, to state incisively those dietetic laws which cannot be violated with impunity.

Infants' foods are put forward *ad nauseam*. The best of these undoubtedly contain certain elements of nutrition combined in proportions somewhat approximating to those which science would dictate. There are not many, however, that we shall be able to class in this category, certainly not half-a-dozen. It would be invidious to point out in detail the full advantages of some of these, but it is necessary in the first place to draw a deep line of demarcation between those foods that are suitable for infants and those others which may be considered better adapted for the use of invalids of more mature years.*

If infants are to be fed at all upon anything to supplement diluted milk or the equivalent of that which they would derive from their mothers, it must be insisted that this supplemental food shall be rendered soluble without necessitating any action either of the saliva or of any of the other juices of the body. The peculiar principle called diastase, which is produced by the malting of grain, causes the transformation of the starchy matters into sugar, which renders them entirely soluble, in which condition alone are they capable of being taken up by the absorbents, and so assimilated.

One or two infants' foods are already before the public, in which these conditions have been duly recognised. The rest of the foods advertised as suitable for infants consist of but little else than cooked or baked flour, in which state ordinary wheat flour is to a very small degree more easy of

---

* In exemplification of this point, we have shown that Liebig's "Food for Infants," as prepared by Messrs. Savory and Moore, contains but very little untransformable starch, while Mr. Mellin carries the malting still further, and renders almost all the starch soluble. "Farina vitæ," on the other hand, is very highly nutritious food for invalids, but is not adapted for very young infants.

digestion. To whatever extent the starchy matters are not capable of conversion by the other principles contained in the food, the starchy constituents must be considered objectionable to all young infants, inasmuch as there is no power in their saliva of transforming this starch.

For this reason we feel bound to protest against the very improper pretensions daily made in the advertisements of certain cornflours. Some of these boldly state the very reverse of the truth, to the effect that their wonderful preparations contain all the essential elements of nutrition, whereas, in fact, they are almost universally found on examination to consist of starch alone. In other words, when prepared with water only, as is directed on the labels of some of these, they contain no nutriment which is assimilable by an infant of less than five or six months of age. If no other food is taken, starvation must inevitably result. This has, unfortunately, occurred in too many instances, as shown by the records of Coroners' and police courts during the last two years.

Where foods of this kind are used by mothers as thickening of diluted milk for young infants, it must be remembered that they cannot digest the starch, and it must become liable to the most objectionable decomposition. We all know how prone infants are to the formation of acidity and wind.

The first is almost invariably that which is denominated lactous, and the second is but the necessary consequence of this fermentation. Both of these usually occur from indigestible starchy matters, when such are present in the food, unless the bowels are so active as to be able to expel the starch unchanged before decomposition can take place. If any mucilaginous matter is required to give to the diluted milk a thicker consistency, and render it, as it is termed, bland, the mucilaginous matter in contradistinction to coagulum afforded by barley-water may be used with advantage.

It can never be repeated too often that milk food is the proper food of all infantile life. If the circumstances under which this is obtainable have been thoroughly investigated, and after due inquiry found to be inadequate to the support of the infant, an inquiry which can never be too fully or too perseveringly carried out before being abandoned, then, and then only, are the best kinds of those truly soluble infants' foods to be advocated. All others must be condemned on the strongest possible grounds ; the evidence upon which that condemnation is based being attested by the best medical evidence of the present day, viz., that the majority of deaths among infants not nurtured upon milk are occasioned by injudicious food substitutes mainly consisting of starch.

CHAPTER IV.

MEAT.

IF food were considered under the ancient description of meat and drink, the meaning of the word meat would be very different from that which we have to discuss. The old adage, "What is meat to some may be poison to others," unfortunately is sometimes true of that portion of our food obtained from the butchers' shops. Many persons, in selecting their daily joint, believe, when they secure the meat which is charged at the highest price, that they obtain the finest possible nourishment.

They may sometimes be correct, they may sometimes also obtain fine flavour, the most juicy condition, and the most tender fibre. The æsthetic enjoyments of carving may be indulged in so as to display at once the dexterity of the carver, the skill of the butcher, and the ripeness of the animal; and, at the same time, a sufficiently scientific veterinary surgeon would pounce down upon the tempting helpings, and declare that that which is most inviting has only been obtained by the degeneration of the most valuable qualities of the meat.

Every one must occasionally notice in the newspapers reports of meat having been seized as unfit for human food. The evidence upon which such meat is condemned is not of such a nature as will bear the strictest scientific investigation. That a large quantity of the meat undoubtedly comes into the market in a condition unfit to be consumed is unfortunately but too true; but we have great reason to fear that the essential points of discriminating between that which is likely to prove absolutely injurious, that which is objectionable, and that which would pass muster, are not yet sufficiently understood, either by the inspectors whose duty it is to investigate these matters, or by the purchasers.

It may appear ridiculous to declare, with some emphasis, that at no time of the year is the liability of purchasing diseased meat so great as immediately after the great cattle shows. Instances, however, have not been wanting to prove that the beasts exhibited have been in that condition in which fat deposited externally, and intersticially (as marbling of the meat), and also in the viscera, has reached such a degree as to admit of the easy passage of the finger through the walls of the pericardium, or membrane which surrounds the heart. Mr. Gant testified that this was the precise condition in which he found several beasts exhibited by the late Prince Consort, the slaughter of which anticipated by a very brief period the inevitable termination of their lives by disease (fatty degeneration).

A very few years ago a London fog of more than usual intensity was found sufficient to destroy the slight vitality of a large number of beasts so exhibited. There was no evidence that other animals in the metropolis, living under ordinary circumstances, and stalled, suffered to any extreme degree from this smoke-laden atmosphere; and the moral pointed by this event seems to be that the unnatural feeding necessary to the production of this mass of flesh, together with the treatment which entirely precluded the exercise necessary to cause free expansion of the lungs—in fact, the forcing system generally adopted—is one which must result in the production of flesh minus vitality, and in food with a minimum of justly balanced nutrition.

In considering the question of the food value of meat, it must be remembered that it supplies a distinct requirement. It is moreover accepted in this position by the instincts of mankind in general, as especially supplying the place of the nitrogenous and muscular elements of food in daily diet. It is not either purchased or used as a substitute for butter or fatty matters, nor can it be economically applied for this purpose.

A very curious calculation might be made as to the amount of fat purchased of the butcher, and paid for as meat, of which a portion is trimmed off by the cook, and a large amount becomes dripping, while of the remainder, that which is left on the plate will show how little is really consumed. The marine store dealer in this instance probably obtains the greatest advantage out of our national desire for fat meat, which is evidently satisfactory to the eye alone. The fat of venison is generally appreciated to the fullest possible extent, because of the scarcity of a due deposit of adipose tissue in an animal so active as the deer. On the other hand, stall-feeding of oxen, and the confining of sheep for feeding purposes, and other means of obtaining an undue development of carcase weight, produce a flabby muscular tissue. Such a deposit as this can only be wasted in the slaughter-house, the kitchen, and on the table.

These same observations apply to the feeding of pigs. Every housekeeper is acquainted with the difference which exists between bacon which swells in the pot, and that which shrinks. This depends upon the solidity of tissue, which is consequent to a certain extent upon the feeding of the animal, and to a small degree upon the peculiar breed.

Diseases of meat present peculiar appearances, sometimes easily recognisable, at others not so obvious. One of the most deadly of these is the presence of encysted parasites known in pork by the scientific name of *trichinæ spiralis*. The dangers incident to the presence of this deadly parasite are only to be overcome by a full cooking temperature equal to that of boiling water. There are various other diseases of animals which render their flesh unsuitable for human food. But the length of time during which meat may be kept short of the production of real putrefaction has yet to be determined as bearing upon its wholesomeness. This is a point to which we have directed attention, and we hope at no distant date to be assured that its dietetic importance is more generally appreciated.

FISH.

The flesh of fish bears a closer resemblance to butchers' meat than is sometimes recognised. Indeed, the analogy between the flesh of sturgeon and veal is sufficiently obvious both in appearance and flavour. The difference between certain kinds of fish having what is termed white flesh and other fish having red or pink flesh will not always afford any indication as to the relative proportion of nutriment which either kind may possess in nitrogenous substance, soluble albuminoid matter, and even less in regard to its constituent of oil. But it may be accepted that those fish which contain the largest quantity of oil are, from that very fact, more liable to prove difficult of digestion.

The fibrinous portion of many descriptions of fish is naturally harder and coarser than the generality of animal flesh. The necessity is, therefore, greater that in cooking every attention should be given to rendering the muscular fibre as tender as possible.

In consequence of some little delicacy being requisite in the preparation of fish for the table, no little prejudice has been excited against it among the labouring classes. It is also supposed to be very inferior to flesh meat in nutriment. This is not the case to the extent supposed, the amount of nitrogenous matter being, on an average, about the same as in lean meat; it is, however, generally less available, as it cannot be kept fresh for the same length of time. Notwithstanding which, if difficulties had not been interposed by those interested in Billingsgate Market, a very large quantity of most valuable food might be daily brought to London, and retailed at the most moderate prices.*

* The establishment of wholesale and retail markets for fish in London has been again and again attempted, and the history of Columbia Market affords one of the most lamentable instances of failure.

Meat.

All efforts to accomplish this have unfortunately up to the present time been frustrated by trade devices, and while thousands throughout the country are suffering in health from the want of that description of nourishment which fish would cheaply afford, thousands of tons of fish are permitted to rot as manure on the sea coast.

CHAPTER V.

VEGETABLES AND FRUIT.

VEGETABLES must be dealt with, for our present purpose of illustration, from a totally different point of view from that in which the botanist, herbalist, or vegetarian would regard them. We have no intention of treating of the vegetable kingdom in general, much less of attempting to give any idea of the food principles peculiar to any very extended series of edible vegetable matters. Some of the commonest of those vegetables which find their way to our tables will be quite sufficient to enable us to point out the leading features which must be thoroughly recognised as appertaining more particularly to this very varied and important group of food substances.

If, for one reason more than another, we should select, even if we were not compelled, a few of the commoner descriptions of vegetables as types, it would be because that vast variety which does exist of vegetable productions suitable for the table is unfortunately almost unattainable in this country. Potatoes, cabbages, onions, carrots, and turnips,

Vegetables and Fruit.

with a few more, express the extreme limits of all that an ordinary greengrocer desires to offer his customers for selection; the rest are luxuries, and must be paid for as such, even if, as is the case with some of the choicest of our salads, they can be obtained by those who seek them at the mere cost of collection.

The potato may, perhaps, be taken as the most generally valuable of our common table vegetables. The natural assumption of food value accorded to the potato depends not only upon its solidity (containing a quarter its weight of solid matters, the remaining three quarters being water), but also from the circumstance that these solids contain no less than 16 or 17 per cent. of starch, and from $1\frac{1}{2}$ to 2 per cent. nitrogenous matter, together with mineral matters of a very varied constitution.

The estimate of the nutrition which this vegetable affords is not entirely to be confined to the properties of its components, but also to the existence of certain dilute acids, citric and phosphoric, which probably cause a remarkable anti-scorbutic effect to be produced by the raw potato. How much of this citric and phosphoric acid is preserved after the process of cooking must depend considerably upon the method adopted. But the hygienic value of potatoes which have neither germinated, nor become changed by long keeping, is more likely to be under than over estimated.

Errors, however, are likely to be perpetrated when the dietetic importance of potatoes is so far misunderstood as to lead persons to believe that it is easy to consume and digest a sufficient amount of this tuber to enable it to become a substitute for more highly nitrogenous and flesh-forming foods. This has had much to do with many of our national difficulties in dealing with Ireland. The hibernian predilection, which has been so well known as to cause potatoes to be termed "Murphys," absolutely caused a famine when better food was offered and rejected.

It may have been a mistake to supply maize, which requires a totally different method of cookery, but we can speak from our own experience of the superiority of well-creed or perfectly swollen rice, drained from superfluous moisture, in the place of potatoes, whenever the latter are diseased, badly grown, or of inferior quality. The green vegetables, such as cabbage, contain too small a proportion of nitrogenous matters to render them an important item for consideration in daily food. But the immense variety of their chemical and physical qualities suggests other values than those to be attributed to the considerable amount of cellulose and vegetable acids.

If, in variety alone, they tempt the appetite or stimulate digestion, both by their alkaloids, flavours, and agreeable crispness when uncooked; so, also, as regarded from an economical point of view "greens" accomplish a result by no means to be despised, in assisting to fill the stomach, so that the mechanical necessities of the digestion are aided in the supplemental action they afford to the more nitrogenous foods.

We must not lose sight of the peculiar principles inherent to the lettuce, asparagus, celery, spinach, watercress, and radish. Some of these are truly medicinal. The volatile principles contained in many of them approximate more closely than might be suspected to those of certain spices and highly stimulative condiments. They should therefore be accepted rather as addenda to any meal than as forming substantial nourishment.

Carrots, parsnips, turnips, and beetroot are roots in which the starchy matters are found already transformed to a considerable extent into sugar from an early period of their growth. Some of these contain fatty matters to a great extent, and all of them possess peculiar flavours due to volatile constituents which exercise different effects upon different individuals. In themselves the saccharine and mineral components are not to be dissociated at the table from the harder ligneous cellulose which form the fibrous structure of those vegetables, which when they are slow-grown renders them extremely difficult of mastication, if not impossible of digestion. On the other hand, a forced growth of extreme rapidity prevents the due development of their higher flavours and saccharine extractives, augmenting principally the watery constituents.

It may be remarked that the development of the distinctive peculiarities and valuable qualities of most vegetables is increased to a very great extent by out-door culture, in the same way as the finest flavours are imparted to fruit by the direct influence of the sun's rays.

A few very enthusiastic individuals have lately thrust themselves into print for the purpose of attempting to demonstrate that man is a frugivorous animal. If they had been content to assert that mankind may be considered as manifesting a strong predilection for fruit, no one would seek to gainsay the palpable truism; but when certain inaccurate delineations of the osteology of the skulls of man, monkeys, and tigers are put forward to prove that man is by nature destined to live upon fruit, it can only be replied that in no part of the world does he do so.

Some years back, during a scarcity of the potato crops, a number of letters appeared in the *Times*, urging that in times gone by the people of Devonshire subsisted chiefly upon apples. When, however, it is shown that apples contain not more than a quarter of the flesh-forming principles of the potato, it must become evident how utterly illogical any such inference must be deemed. Pleasant, agreeable, and wholesome as ripe, fresh, well-grown fruit undoubtedly is to the majority of healthy persons, the cooling and laxative properties possessed by certain descriptions are those to which the greatest value must be accorded. Taken broadly, fruit is not food; but the question of its use for any such purpose need scarcely be discussed, as we are strongly of opinion that no one, unless compelled to do so for a time, has ever attempted to make use of it for this purpose.

Here the plea for vegetarianism must be impartially considered from the same aspect. The pretensions put forward are almost invariably incorrectly stated, their postulate being that man not only can, but should, subsist entirely upon vegetables and fruit. No one can doubt that life may be maintained for a considerable period upon the breadstuffs and other vegetable products, without the use of any matters of animal origin whatever. In eastern countries the food of certain religious sects may be said to be mainly vegetable; but without refining upon the point, how far it is exclusively so, or what are the conditions of the people so fed, we have to regard, not only what can be done, but what has been done, to maintain this theory.

In this and other countries enthusiasts have ridden their hobbies as hard upon vegetarianism as upon any crude theory, whether of morality, religion, or dietetics. But in no work that we are acquainted with has it ever been seriously proposed that vegetarianism, pure and simple, should even be introduced.

If we accept the cookery books which seek to allure us from our animal foods and other so-called abominations, we find that the sum total of animal matters introduced into vegetarian cookery exceeds in food value those in the dietetic scale adopted in many of our most successful public institutions throughout the country. In fact, what with milk, eggs, butter, and cheese, animal matters are employed to an extent which far surpasses that procurable by many of the poorer classes of this and other countries, whose greatest desire is to obtain as much animal food as possible.

But if vegetarian cookery books are unconsciously frank in demonstrating their total want of consistency, those who uphold the use of vegetables alone are usually found to be still more egregious in the manner in which they actually carry their theories into practice. Dr. W. B. Carpenter estimated the average quantity of non-vegetable food consumed in the house of a friend of his, professing these untenable principles, to be considerably in excess of the animal food consumed by the members of his own household.

The crude notions of monomaniacs on these subjects occasion, fortunately, but little injury, while they merely essay to demonstrate the effects upon their own persons; nature is almost invariably sufficiently powerful in its impulses to prevent them from undermining their constitutions by any too strict adhesion to their particular fancies. It is only when children, invalids, and others unable to select for themselves are forced and compelled to eke out what little nourishment they can obtain from purely vegetable sources, that it becomes necessary to step in with the authoritative declaration that a vegetarian diet pure and simple is utterly unsuited for the nutrition of man.

CHAPTER VI.

FOOD ACCESSORIES.

MANY articles of consumption which cannot be termed food, but which yet contain principles either essential for the digestion of food, or stimulative to assist in that digestion, may be enumerated as food accessories, and one absolutely necessary to life cannot conveniently otherwise be classified. Of course, we allude to common salt (chloride of sodium).

The peculiar type of individuals who find comfort in the belief that they have discovered some wonderful virtue in the total abstention from animal foods or from alcoholic drinks, occasionally find vent for their eccentricities in endeavouring to do altogether without salt, and more particularly in promulgating their notions upon this craze; others eat salt in enormous quantities with the greater portion of their food, evidently without being aware that a sufficient quantity of it can be swallowed to produce results of a very dangerous nature.

A morbid appetite for the excessive use of salt is only another form of that depraved condition which incites a desire to partake largely of matters which a healthy instinct would avoid, as certainly as if the noxious consequences had been fully explained. An instance of this kind occurred within our own experience, in which a woman continued for some years to eat dry uncooked flour in considerable quantities, sometimes as much as a tea-cupful at a time. Indeed, a peculiar tendency appears to exist among idiots and maniacs for the swallowing of any little miscellaneous unconsidered trifles with ostrich-like avidity, and in some countries an infatuation for dirt eating (not metaphorically) has become so great, that hundreds, who cannot be restrained from this strange gratification, fall victims to the effects of a diseased imagination, producing a wasting of bodily powers by this means.

The use of salt, then, may be safely regulated by a healthy instinct. But the necessity for salt may be explained by the composition of the gastric juice. The most powerful solvent acid which insures the digestion of food is that known as hydrochloric. This is furnished entirely by the amount of salt, either chloride of sodium or potassium, taken with the food, or naturally contained in it. Unless a large quantity of this acid is present in the gastric juice, the other digestive principles are inert, or are not given out during the passage of food through the stomach.

Nothing more need be urged to show the vital necessity for a sufficiency of salt accompanying the daily food. But it is somewhat curious to note how many persons declare that they do not take salt, on the plea, among others, of its being in some way mysteriously connected with original sin and all the consequent evils that flesh is heir to.

These, perhaps otherwise sane individuals, appear to be unaware that most mixed food contains a certain proportion of salt, and the objection to it can therefore be one of degree only, as is the case with alcohol, with which we shall presently have to deal at length. Without laying down any hard and fast line with regard to the amount of salt required to be taken with the daily food, we can only suggest that it must bear some approximate relation to the amount of flesh-forming food which has to be digested by the gastric juice.

Vinegar (acetic acid) may undoubtedly rank next to salt as a valuable food accessory. When taken in small quantities, this acid, if not too strong, which is usually the fault of the more expensive malt vinegars, exercises a digestive influence upon the gelatinous constituent of the harder portion of the meat. The total quantity of vinegar consumed in this country is so immensely greater than is usually supposed, that we have to think for a moment as to the form in which it is chiefly taken. There can be no doubt that cold meat creates a demand for some such solvent, and the pickles, so largely consumed by the lower classes with cheese and other food, and by those in better circumstances with cold meat, supply this requirement, in addition, also, to affording an increased stimulus to the digestive organs from the various peppers and spices which they contain.

In the same way, salad-dressing of vinegar and oil enables uncooked vegetable matter to be digested by thousands who could not tolerate raw vegetables without it; the acidity of the vinegar being counteracted to some extent by the smoothness of the oil, while the oil is rendered more palatable by the vinegar, and in addition to its food value acts as a mechanical lubricant to the intestines.

Mustard possesses not only stimulating properties, but is a valuable tonic and excitant. When largely diluted, it becomes an emetic, as most persons are aware; but it is peculiar to this condiment, that unless mixed with water, the sharp aromatic pungency is not developed. For this reason the acid preparation of mustard used by the French and Germans possesses little of the powerful flavour of that which we are accustomed to use in this country.

Even if mustard be mixed with wine containing as much alcohol as common sherry, the volatile oil which gives it its full strength is not developed; for, be it understood, the pungency of mustard is the result of the peculiar fermentation which takes place immediately a sufficient quantity of water is added to it.

Peppers are of two kinds, those which are properly spices, such as black pepper and the white which is derived from it; the others, such as the different kinds of capsicum from which red peppers are produced, are derived from pods dried and ground—that which is by far the most largely used in this country, of course, being the former.

The effects of these are carminative, anti-spasmodic, and stimulant, affording some little relief in cases of deranged functions, especially with regard to the digestion of vegetables, and they also form a pleasant seasoning when used in small quantities in the various culinary operations.

Red peppers are more directly stimulating, and, at the same time, may be considered in some instances as irritants. Where the lining membrane of the bowels is in a state of relaxation, as in summer diarrhœa, the action of this pepper is more directly astringent. This action is only produced when administered occasionally. If habitually taken, cayenne pepper produces a congested condition of the whole alimentary canal, and, particularly, engorgement of the liver. In all cases of congestive dyspepsia, highly seasoned food should be avoided.

All kinds of pepper seem the most approved of when taken with those articles of food which demand the accompaniment of salt. But other stimulants of considerable activity appear to blend pleasantly with those kinds of food which contain or are combined with sugar. These are the spices known as such, and although their uses are better appreciated in Eastern countries, perhaps, than at home, still we all recognise the important aid, culinary and gustative, which they afford when delicately handled.

Unfortunately, cooks incompetent to the development of the more subtle flavours of their materials disguise the poverty of their resources with a superabundance of the contents of the spice box. All harmony of flavour is thus destroyed, and the digestive advantages which a moderate amount of spice undoubtedly confers are lost in the nausea which they occasion.

CHAPTER VII.

BEER.

WE may commence the subject of alcoholic stimulants with that which in this country and in the colder climates has the largest consumption. Not being a wine-producing country, nor one in which spirits are mainly depended upon, beer, or the immediate product of fermented liquors, is that which must be considered the staple product, best suited to the tastes and requirements of the climate. Beer, as we have known it in our own personal experience, is a very different article from that which was in vogue one or two generations ago.

As we shall have to revert to the beers of the present day in the endeavour to point out to what degree they are suitable generally, or more or less so in particular instances, we may touch upon the beers of the past to show the progress that has been made, not only in the public taste, but in the brewing of beers, which have from time to time followed the demands of greater intelligence on the part of the consumers. So stimulated to the production of more suitable beverages, that recognition of progressive superiority which is the reward of foresight in commercial enterprise has been obtained.

Until the production of the pale ales, which were first exported to India as being more suitable on account of their lightness and less alcoholicity, strong beers of every kind were more easily brewed and better appreciated than beer of a delicate and lighter description, and until it became fashionable to believe that everything bitter was a valuable tonic, few persons would have cared to indulge in that excess of hop flavour which was necessary to keep season-brewed beers over the summer, in which the extractive matters were so much reduced.

At that time, what were termed vatted ales, porter, or stout, were alone to be relied on, and to enable beer to stand one or two years in the vat, these were first brewed to contain the maximum of extract of malt, so as to leave, after fermentation, a considerable body of saccharine matter, which would sustain a slight secondary fermentation for an almost indefinite period. Acidity meant then something much more nearly approaching vinegar than that which we are accustomed to complain of in the present day. In fact, what was termed hardness would represent an acetous condition of beer quite undrinkable according to the present tastes.

The only difference between that kind of beer which was ready for consumption soon after being brewed, and those which were termed stock ales, consisted in the former somewhat resembling what we now call mild ale, and the latter being brewed to so much greater strength as to enable it to keep without becoming absolutely sour. We are not alluding to table or small beer, which washy and unpalatable decoctions were scarcely more than the rinsings of the mash-tub or the results of injudicious home-brews. We are rather concerned to notice those beers which were of highest repute, and acquired the highest prices. These may be briefly divided into two classes—new beers and old beers; the one being sweet, clammy, and almost repulsive from the heavy loading of saccharine and other extractive matter, only slightly fermented out, and therefore prone to carry on fermentation in the stomach, and to produce the well-known train of symptoms termed heartburn, acidity, flatulence, etc.

The other, almost valued by its age like port wine, was not despised, if in addition to the strongest possible alcoholicity it contained compound ethers and acids sufficient to render it highly intoxicating; so that the beer-drinkers of the so-called fine old ales had generally sufficient respect for their potency to drink them out of very small glasses, and usually in moderate quantities.

These beers were sipped rather than drunk, and deep draughts or thirst-assuaging potations must have been supplied from the small beers rather than from those which appeared to excite their greatest admiration.

It is a very singular circumstance, even at the present time, to find that the intoxicating qualities of different kinds of stimulants are so little understood that they are almost invariably referred to as being due to the per-centage of alcohol present. If anything could show the fallacy of this rough-and-ready estimate of their inebriating constituents, it would be the well-known effect of a small quantity of the old and strong ale.

By the common analysis which is supposed to gauge the amount of alcohol, and which may be quite sufficient for excise purposes, the per-centage of proof spirit would not probably exceed fifteen or sixteen per cent., less, in fact, than the proportional alcohol of the purest and weakest French wines.

Few persons are, we should imagine, liable to become prostrated by a pint bottle of any of the wines which are imported under the shilling duty. A pint of old ale, however, which has been long enough in the cellar to develop the acids and ethers before alluded to, is more than sufficient to upset the equilibrium of some of the strongest of those who drink beer habitually. When these facts came to be recognised as being utterly incompatible with the consumption of beer in hot climates, a very successful attempt was made to counteract the bad effect of keeping and transport by increasing the amount of hops, while the amount of malt extract was simultaneously lowered. Beer was by this means exported to India which was more adapted for its requirements; and as its success was everywhere apparent, as contrasted with the stronger and more alcoholic beers sent out previously, greater virtues were perhaps attributed to the bitterness than at any time properly belonged to its tonic effects.

From India the taste for the thinner bitter ales was brought back to this country, and for many years bitter beers were considered a kind of panacea for want of appetite, loss of digestive power, and many other deranged conditions with which it had no relation. A sort of false appetite for bitterness was stimulated, and less attention was paid to the other valuable characteristics of beer than to the two fashionable requirements—that of paleness and excess of hop flavour.

At this time the pale ales of Burton came prominently to the fore. The peculiarity of the water of that locality prevented the extraction of some of the less desirable constituents of the malt, and at the same time extracted only the finer and less acrid bitters of the hop, so as to develop in the beer the aroma of the hop oils rather than that of the hop resin. The natural peculiarity of the Burton water has had a most valuable tendency towards controlling the inordinate desire for overbitterness, until by natural selection that portion of the public capable of appreciating the superiority of Burton beer began to set their faces against the coarse, heavy, bitter beers which had been so widely recommended and consumed.

It would be utterly impossible to enter upon the *minutiæ* of the process of brewing, as at present carried on; suffice it to say that ales brewed with soft water are almost inadmissible on account of their liability to develop considerable quantities of lactic, acetic, and other objectionable acids, while, on the other hand, the resinous matter of the hop, giving to them the coarse harsh bitter, which dwells upon the tongue, cannot but be considered an injurious astringent, if the beer containing it is regularly partaken of.

We have not hesitated to recognise the value of light ales other than those of Burton, but in all cases where these have been found to come up to fair standards of dietetic excellence, they must have been brewed with good and pure water containing or having artificially introduced the equivalent of the salts of the Burton springs.

The essentials of good wholesome ale may be briefly enumerated: a moderate strength, not exceeding from 9 to 12 per cent. of proof spirit, only a sufficiency of extractive left in the beer to enable it to retain its life, briskness, and a mellow and evanescent bitterness preponderating but slightly over the sweeter flavours of the malt.

It is, in fact, a happy combination of those flavours which constitutes the perfection of all lighter ales. What are now termed mild ales should not differ very greatly from what we have described, except that less hop is used. These milder beers, again, with age, acquire certain delicate ethers of a less pronounced character than those which were formerly held in esteem.

We now come to another kind of beer, in which the distinctive peculiarities are attained by the use of high-dried or black malt. These have been always produced in great perfection in the vicinity of London, and some of the breweries chiefly devoted to the brewing of stout and porter date back nearly a couple of centuries. The word stout seems to imply, and no doubt did convey with considerable accuracy, the notion that it contained as large a proportion as could conveniently be introduced into it of the solid matters of the malt; in some kinds the soluble extractive amounts to more than 25 per cent. This would no doubt ferment, and become extremely objectionable, if it were not for the antiseptic influence of certain portions of the malt, which has been acquired by the process of drying at a very high temperature.

But if properly prepared, extracts of malt for black or brown beers should be less liable to after-fermentation than that used for the stronger ales. With these, again, the keeping qualities of the hop are not so essential as when pale malt is used. If, therefore, brewers of London porter and stout use, as they do, fine hops, it is rather to improve the flavour of their beer, than to overcome the effects of any probable decomposition. For some time past somewhat thinner stout has been preferred, and with good reason; and so a beer somewhat between porter and stout has been put forward as being suitable for general requirements.

Why it should be necessary to designate light stout "cooper," we cannot say; but this designation seems to convey some particular blend of the two best qualities of porter and stout, and it is undoubtedly superior, when brewed directly to the desired strength, than when stout and porter are mixed together in the rough-and-ready manner in which this compound beverage was originally prepared, namely, by drawing the two constituents from the separate barrels as received from the breweries; and is to be preferred, where quick draught can be assured, to similar beer which has been bottled.

But the difficulty which always exists in small families drawing their own beer is, first of all, a loss of the carbonic acid which constitutes the so-called briskness or life in the beer, and the disposition which accompanies this loss of carbonic acid gas, and the introduction of air into the barrel, namely, the commencement of acetous fermentation, which in time changes the beer into vinegar. Then, again, the stirring up of the sediment of the beer, by the beer engines of the publicans, necessitates the use of finings to throw down and precipitate these matters in such a form as they will not easily cloud the beer. For this purpose, gelatine dissolved in sour beer or crude acetic acid is very commonly used, and cannot be considered otherwise than detrimental to the beer.

The difficulty, also, of getting beer into good condition in cellars where the temperature cannot be properly regulated, renders beer kept under these disadvantages flat, cloudy, and altogether unsatisfactory. For these reasons a considerable quantity of beer is bottled, even for a rapid consumption, and there is a decided advantage to many persons in being able to keep a beer immediately available, which it would not be if it had to be stored in barrels which can only be kept in proper cellars.

Here, however, we enter upon that which constitutes a large trade in itself, and is one that requires more knowledge and care than is usually supposed. An objection to bottled beer has been more or less prevalent, in consequence, first of all, of the large amount of carbonic acid gas which is generated after bottling, and of the presence, also, to a greater or less degree, of other acids, chiefly acetic, which are likely to be produced in bottled beers during the process of flattening which all beer has to undergo before bottling.

Generally, beer bottling cannot be considered to be sufficiently well understood, or carried out with the requisite care, to prevent very unequal results. There are, however, some firms who devote themselves especially to this branch of industry, and undeviating attention, scrupulous cleanliness, and great discrimination in the beers they purchase, enable them to send out bottled beers of almost invariable excellence. We have been much surprised to find that in certain hands the science of beer bottling has been brought to such a point of perfection, that almost every bottle may be relied on as sound and in proper condition.*

The difference between the introduction of carbonic acid gas in large quantities in soda-water, and that conveyed into the digestive organs by the medium of beer at high pressure, is easily marked by the after effects. In the first place, distention by flatus is frequently removed with great rapidity by the eruptive escape of the gas almost as soon as it is swallowed. When bottled beers are highly charged with this gas, particularly in the case of stout, the large amount of saccharine and other extractives carries the carbonic acid beyond the stomach into the bowels, producing that great and unpleasant distention which renders these bottled beers inadmissible in a large number of cases.

But if this mechanical condition were the only drawback, less objection might be taken to the general use of bottled beer, than when a considerable quantity of acetic and lactic acids are also present, inasmuch as these betoken a continued fermentative action which not only carries the amount of carbonic acid then present into the

* Messrs. Newman and Son furnished samples of their "Dietetic Stout," which we submitted to the most trying vicissitudes of temperature for nearly six months, yet proved on testing to be quite sound.

bowels, but proceeds to generate there a vast quantity more of it.

Although beer may be regarded as being our national beverage, several points must be taken into consideration in forming an opinion as to the quantity which may be beneficially consumed by people during different periods of life. The most prominent of these, undoubtedly, are constitutional temperament and general habits, especially, with regard to the amount of exercise taken. In childhood, unquestionably, much benefit is often obtained by the use of small quantities of light and sound beer; but although this is of special value in the case of delicate children, where from want of appetite they are indisposed to take a sufficiency of their ordinary food, still it must not be argued that during the earlier years of life any stimulant is generally advisable.

But if in individual cases a stimulant appears necessary, without doubt, in the majority of instances, beer is preferable to wine. It need hardly be pointed out that spirits are, in no case, to be administered in lieu of beer. Beer certainly does introduce peculiar constituents of food matter, altogether independent of the amount of alcohol contained in it, and, in some instances, these are of extreme value, and can hardly be so advantageously or readily assimilated in any other form.

In addition to this, the gentle stimulant increases both the desire for other food, and also the power of digesting it. In one particular regard, the administration of malt-saccharine by means of beer tends directly to the solution and digestion of the other starchy portions of the food. In this manner it greatly assists the function of the salivary glands, and, perhaps, that of the pancreatic fluid. Too little recognition has been bestowed upon the importance of this healthy fermentative action.

Passing from the period of childhood to that of the rapid growth of youth, where, in addition to the strain put upon the system in the formation of new tissue, a very large amount of exercise is usually and advantageously taken, beer, if it cannot be regarded accurately as food, distinctly occupies the place of a most important adjuvant, stimulating nervous power, and assisting assimilation, together with the consequent formation of the various structures of the body.

Good sound beer, in moderate quantities, may be regarded as something more than the mere saccharine which may be taken up. When it is instinctively and generally desired, its value should not be under-estimated, nor should it be withheld when no distinct evidence is shown of its producing any ill effects in the shape of inflammatory or congestive mischief. In all instances, however, strict moderation must be observed.

In adult life, persons having sedentary occupations can only take a small quantity of beer daily with benefit. Whereas those who live much in the open air, and take a large amount of exercise, are able to consume comparatively large quantities of this beverage with apparent impunity, although, in either case, the benefit is by no means so certain as when a well-regulated allowance is adhered to. Whenever a large amount of rich food, together with wines and spirits, are habitually taken, the loaded or congested condition of the liver and other organs of elimination, generally produced by these habits, renders the taking of beer in any quantity highly injurious, tending, as it does, to the excessive formation of uric acid, the presence of which, in excess, constitutes the condition generally known as gout.

There is no reason to suppose that the popular notion of beer being productive of rheumatism and gout, when a moderate and proper diet is adhered to, is correct, unless the beer be taken in very large quantities; and, therefore, according to the most enlightened opinions of the present time, there is no necessity to abstain altogether from malt liquors during an attack of these diseases.

In cases where there is a distinct tendency to

calculous deposits, beer is certainly not admissible. In old age it is, also, scarcely to be recommended; the impaired powers and feeble digestion, requiring stimulants, need those which are more readily diffused and absorbed. There are, however, many old persons of hale and hearty constitutions who can take beer as easily as they can take other food.

CHAPTER VIII.

WINE.

IN the fermentation of beer, for the production of a certain amount of alcohol, it is always necessary to introduce a more rapid and vigorous ferment than naturally exists in malted grain, from which beer is brewed. In grape juice, whether pressed from unripe, ripe, or over-ripe grapes, a certain amount of natural ferment is always present, which is sufficient to set up that alcoholic fermentation which, when carried out under suitable conditions, results in wine of different kinds, according to the nature of the grape, the soil, and the climate in which it is grown.

It is only within certain limits of temperature that vines produce such grapes as are best adapted to wine-making, or, in other words, in which the true vinous fermentation is naturally produced of sufficient strength to counteract and prevent the working of other ferments, which are invariably objectionable, and sometimes fatal to the wines in which they germinate in any quantities.

If we take a line through Europe, a little north of the Rhine district, extending eastward, the wine-growing zone may be considered to be comprised in the southern portion. From the more luscious and highly saccharine wines of the south, which are pressed from grapes affording the strongest vinous fermentation, owing to the excess of sugar, to the thinner and more delicate wines of France and Germany, where the chief difficulty is to prevent formation of acetic acid, from the want of sufficient saccharine to enable the fermentation to proceed with a rapidity which ensures soundness, every description of grape is attempted to be made into wine. In addition to these varieties of materials for wine-making, there is a still greater distinction in the different products, according to the skill of the grower, the after-treatment, and the other circumstances above mentioned.

To so great an extent has the classification of wine proceeded, that it is utterly impossible, within the space devoted to our present consideration of the subject, to do more than furnish certain typical illustrations of a few of the more ordinary descriptions of wine in common use.

We must proceed south for the exemplification of the strongest natural wines. Those of Portugal, Spain, Italy, and Greece, varying always among themselves according to the situation of the vineyard, may be said to include that extreme of alcoholic fermentation which can be naturally wrought out from grape juice, without any other treatment except pressing and allowing it to stand at certain temperatures during its fermentation.

From a vast number of analyses of wines, well ascertained to be altogether free from added spirit, it may be assumed that the highest average alcoholicity does not exceed 26 per cent. of proof. In some rare instances we have found these limits exceeded by some two or three per cent. But a hard and fast line of 26 per cent. of proof spirit, under which the minimum duty of one shilling is charged, cannot be definitely considered as marking the extremity of natural alcoholic fermentation in wine; and, therefore, if some natural wines come in under the half-crown duty, by containing a small amount more alcohol than that permitted, they should not be stigmatised as having been necessarily fortified.

If, however, we are content to agree that 22 or 23 per cent. of proof spirit is the general alcoholicity of the strongest natural wines, we are enabled to afford some estimate of the amount of fortification which these wines have been subjected to when the analysis shows our importations to contain a larger amount.

In all cases, natural wines shipped to this country

without fortification, whether coming from Spain or Portugal, differ considerably from the ordinary sherries and ports of commerce, resembling rather the stronger wines of France and Greece. These natural wines, when made with sufficient experience and care, matured under competent supervision, and shipped at the proper season of the year, present to the palate attractions of a very refined description—the true and perfect vinous flavour, the bouquet of ripe grape ethers, and the characteristic refreshing quality which no wine can possess when heavily fortified.

The natural acids, sometimes toned down, neutralised, or precipitated, by chemical treatment, should be distinctively marked, but there is no necessity whatever for their being associated with the acetic acid produced by bad fermentation which is the result of a decomposition, at once injurious to the keeping qualities of the wine, and to its value as a dietetic.

We may be asked at this point, why a very little acetic acid or vinegar should be considered objectionable in wine, or injurious to the stomach. In the first place, it indicates an unsoundness which must tend to increase until the wine becomes worthless before it can mature. In the second, the acetous fermentation which it betokens is of the self-producing nature, and is carried on in the stomach, among the other constituents of food, after the wine is drunk. On the other hand, a considerable constituent of tartaric acid, the natural acid of the grape in the wine, can be generally tolerated, and a certain amount of this acid is essential to the development of every true vinous flavour.

All things considered, we should prefer of the stronger wines those which contain no adventitious spirit, and among such, some of the Greek, Italian, Spanish, and Portuguese wines are worthy to be laid down in bottle; for within a few years they attain a maturity, flavour, and bouquet, which entitles them to rank among the highest class of wines.

The word maturity has here to be considered as the product of a continuous but very gentle and insensible fermentative change, by which the natural alcohol, in the presence of extractive matters and acids, develops odorous aldehydes and ethers, and precipitates out the surplus tannates and tartrates. In some wines are formed what is termed crust, in others a small flocculent sediment. But in every case where the wine is originally sound, or free from acetous fermentation, and unbrandied, it is invariably improved by keeping, and reaches its perfection in from three to ten or twelve years.

This applies only to the stronger natural wines.

In many instances the wine is made from good grapes, yet, from peculiarities but little understood, it cannot be shipped safely without the addition of a small amount of alcohol, and this is more necessary in certain wines of very hot climates, seeing the temperature is that most favourable for acetous fermentation. Three or four per cent. of alcohol is added at different times, before it arrives in the wine merchants' hands, where it is vatted or blended according to the traditions of the particular firm or the prevalent taste of the different markets.

This moderate addition of grape spirit of good quality is not to be confounded with the heavy fortification of poor, thin, and unsound wines with coarse raw grain, or potato spirit, so generally adopted to arrest the further formation of acetic acid, and to conceal the presence of that which already exists; and it is lamentable to be obliged to confess that the discrimination of, we are afraid, the majority of the public is so little to be depended upon, that they almost seem to prefer those inferior and highly fortified wines to the delicate and exquisite products of the natural fermentation of the grape.

A great outcry has been made with regard to what is termed the chemistry of sherries, and from the public discussion of the subject it has become apparent to us that extremely crude notions are rife. The unscientific readers of the public journals have been led to believe, on the one hand, that plaster of Paris remains as such in wine so treated, while those who can boast of a further insight into chemistry are invited to believe that by certain chemical processes wines can be "deplastered."

But as the real nature of the decomposition which takes place on the addition of plaster (gypsum or sulphate of lime) to wines, which must naturally contain potassium tartrate, can only leave sulphate of potash with a certain amount of tartrates in solution, while it precipitates tartrate of lime; it is evident that only traces of lime can remain in solution, and therefore, there can be, practically, no plaster present to which objection can be taken.

Others dilate on the small quantity of sulphate of potash which is thus dissolved in the wine, and declare that it is unwholesome in itself, and that it injures the wine. We cannot believe that the very minute quantity of sulphate of potash, which can have but a very slight effect, can be really prejudicial, but it certainly must, to some extent, destroy the natural flavour of the wine. Unfortunately, the factitious dryness and other distinctive characteristics of much of the sherry sold is due to the addition of other ingredients far more obnoxious than sulphate of potash.

We need not enumerate the many nostrums which are recommended for this purpose; suffice it to say that the natural so-called dry flavour of fine wine may be considered rather the negative quality of the absence of saccharine, than the positive flavour of astringency and dryness imported into it by the added matters.

Before proceeding to the lighter wines of France and Germany, we cannot pass over the two important types of wine known as Port and Madeira. The basis of port is the fine full-bodied red wine, approaching most nearly, perhaps, to the heavy wines of Bordeaux and Burgundy. It has, however, a much greater astringency than the generality of these, and is known in Portugal as wine that is grown in the Alto Douro. Such wine is usually fortified with a little grape spirit, after the process of the first fermentation.

When it arrives in the hands of the Oporto merchants, it is again strengthened with more spirit, until, from the generally accepted desire on the part of the English consumer, it contains so large a proportion of alcohol, that it requires far greater age in wood or in bottle than any other wine which is imported into this country. Hence the high price which old bottled vintage ports always command.

We may remark that the finest samples of port

wine with which we are acquainted have so far lost the large excess of additional alcohol, that by the time they have arrived at perfection they do not contain more than some seven degrees proof spirit beyond that of the natural wine.

Madeira would not have claimed our attention some few years back, owing to the successive failures of the vines of the island ; but within the last three or four years the improvement in the culture has been such, that, probably, at no period in the history of these vintages have finer wines been shipped to this country than are now daily arriving.

This wine, as most people are aware, is one of the most luscious in flavour. Its peculiar richness is produced, first, by climate, and secondly, by the grapes being allowed to remain on the vines for a very much longer period than is usual in most other countries, except, perhaps, Greece. With these wines the entire per-centage of added spirit amounts to about five per cent. prior to shipment, a very small addition in comparison to many other wines. From its greater body, it is a wine which requires a long keeping to render it agreeable to connoisseurs. The changes which are effected in the extractives, although slowly developed, dispose of considerable proportions of the sweetness, and at the same time bring out the aroma and the delicate qualities so much prized in wines of this class.

The wines of France, which we can now touch upon, are those of Burgundy, Bordeaux, and Epernay. The greater fulness and alcoholic strength of the wines of Burgundy place them next in the category to port and sherry. Some Burgundies have maintained high repute, and sell for prices which are almost prohibitory. But in these, as well as in the other red wines of this district more available for general consumption, there is a peculiarity by no means easy of description or explanation as regards its stimulative properties. It is generally agreed that the strong wines of Burgundy are heating, to a degree, far beyond their alcoholicity.

The white wines, however, have not this effect. Some of these are marvellous examples of perfection, but the cheaper varieties are not generally made with sufficient care to enable them to bear their transport, and the consequence is that an enormous quantity of unsound wine of this description is daily finding its way into this country.

The red wines of Bordeaux, generally comprised under the generic term of claret, constitute a special class of themselves, descending, by infinite gradations, from some of the finest wines in the world down to the thin, poor, but highly astringent inky vinegar so commonly retailed in the grocers' shops. Vintage wines of Château Lafitte, Margaux, Latour, and other renowned vineyards command the admiration of all who can afford to purchase them; but the quantities which are produced in the best years from these vineyards is infinitesimally small, as compared with the wines sold under such denominations, and it is a matter of extreme difficulty to become possessed of more than a few dozen, no matter how high the price paid.

Good Bordeaux wine of medium character, pleasant in taste, and wholesome in effect, could be shipped to this country in sufficient abundance to satisfy all ordinary demands, at prices which should not necessarily debar its use among the middle classes. But with the present rage for excessive cheapness, red wines of all kinds, from many countries, and in varying degrees of unsoundness, are blended and treated so as to conceal their defects for a time, and under the name of claret the very economical section of the community try to persuade themselves that they are drinking wine, when, in truth, they cannot obtain anything that deserves the title for the price.

Epernay furnishes us with the most approved example of the white wine which is bottled before fermentation is completed, and after undergoing various processes by which the carbonic acid gas is retained, reaches us in the form of sparkling wine. Other districts grow wine almost equal to the Epernay standard, and in many years no advantage can be said to be distinguishable between the sparkling wines of Epernay and several other districts.

Beyond the cultivation of a certain class of grape, and its successful pressing and fermentation, the manufacture of champagne depends to an extraordinary degree upon the skill of the bottler. The time and labour which is necessarily occupied during the various processes of disgorgement of the sediment formed in bottling the wine, and the liqueuring and final corking, together with the loss from the bursting of bottles, inevitably raises the cost, and it is absolutely impossible that wines, in reality champagnes, can be sold in this country at the price at which some so purporting are offered.

Sparkling wine, however, may be pleasant and wholesome, and satisfy all the requirements of any but the most fastidious, if a sound wine and adequate knowledge are insisted on. There is no reason, therefore, why good sparkling wine should not be obtainable at moderate prices. Indeed, we have had samples in which the most careful analysis failed to detect the presence of any injurious matters, and which must be considered as wholesome, and are undoubtedly pleasant wines. We are glad to observe that there is a growing taste for the drier and lighter descriptions of sparkling wines, in which the presence of a minimum of liqueur is not sufficient to prevent the immediate detection of any inferiority of the wine.

German wines, such as are represented by those of the Rhine Provinces, generally known by the name of hock, are extremely light and high-flavoured wines. The peculiarity of the finer qualities of these consists in the wonderful development of bouquet and flavour, together with a slight amount of spirituous strength and extractive.

When Rhenish and other German wines are in the slightest degree unsound, very little real flavour and natural aroma is produced, and the ingenuity of wine-growers is continually brought into play to foist upon the public inferior wines which have been flavoured and made up to resemble others of a better character. The selection of wholesome German wine necessitates considerable critical acumen; but in those years when the vintages are good, a plentiful supply of wine of excellent quality is obtainable at moderate prices, and to many persons these light and refreshing wines are peculiarly agreeable during the summer months.

From this brief sketch of the most important wines in general consumption, it will be readily understood that for dietetic purposes they must be divided into three distinct classes. The stronger wines, such as port, sherry, madeira, and Burgundy, are to be regarded as wines for occasional use, and may therefore be rather looked upon in the light of liqueurs. For ordinary daily consumption, wines of lighter character and less alcoholicity, such as Bordeaux, hock, and the less alcoholic wines of Spain, are to be preferred.

The fallacy of drinking those containing nearly 40 per cent. of proof spirit is evident when we consider that the highest amount of alcohol which can be formed in wine only amounts to some 26 or 28 per cent. Ardent spirits are not usually taken without dilution with water to a much greater extent, and in an ordinary glass of whisky or brandy and water there is not more than 15 per cent. of proof spirit.

Many people have been for years in the habit of drinking sherry and port containing the per-centage of alcohol above mentioned, who would have strongly objected to drink spirit and water, from the mistaken idea that they were taking in the wine a weaker fluid than the spirit and water would have been.

The great value of the sparkling wines, apart from their pleasant and exhilarating qualities, chiefly consists in the small per-centage of alcohol which these wines contain, but, from the presence of the carbonic acid with which the wine is charged, the spirit is rendered much more speedily diffusible, so as to produce a greater stimulating effect than the taking of far larger quantities of any alcoholic fluid would be without the presence of this gas. It is for this reason, coupled with the ease with which it is retained in the stomach in many diseases in which sickness forms a prominent feature, that its value is now so generally recognised by physicians in their treatment.

In selecting wines for consumption with meals, it may be broadly taken that white wines are more easily digestible by most persons than the red. The presence of an excess of tannin produces an astringent action which has a tendency to impede digestion of other food in the stomach; but from the same cause the red wines generally considered suitable for dessert are in fact so, the earlier stages of digestion being then completed. It must not, however, be supposed that all white wines are suitable for dinner wines, those which contain the smallest amount of saccharine matters being better adapted for this purpose than wines of a sweeter character. This is the reason why many people are unable to drink certain champagnes with their dinners, on account of the heavy liqueuring which these wines frequently undergo.

At no period, so much as at present, has it been necessary to exercise caution in the selection of wines for dietetic purposes, and although, perhaps, there never was so much good wine to be purchased at so low a price, yet, certainly, there never was so large an amount of worthless, sophisticated, and unwholesome trash absolutely glutting the market.

If the difference between a high-class wine, the excellence of which has been at all times recognised, and the vile imitations with which it has been attempted to simulate these, can be always traced by their immediate effects; so in a much wider ratio we can perceive the cumulative effect upon health induced by the consumption of unsound wine, as compared with the benefit derivable from wines of wholesome character even at the same price.*

* Characteristic samples of the different wines were furnished for analysis by Messrs. Burn and Turner, the Pure Wine Company, Messrs. Rutherford and Co., Messrs. J. L. Denman and Co., Messrs. Stapleton and Co., and others.

CHAPTER IX.

SPIRITS.

DISTILLED spirits occupy a very different place in the dietetic scale from that of fermented beverages. Beer, as we have seen, is produced by the addition of a special ferment, which has nothing whatever to do with the natural fermentation which would occur in the aqueous extract of malt. Wine, on the other hand, requires no added ferment beyond that which it naturally contains to produce a certain amount of alcoholic strength, which will conduce to its own preservation, and to the development of those finer flavours common to all sound fermented beverages which have been kept until they are fully matured.

Spirits are those portions of any fermented saccharine fluid selected, which, being volatile, are carried over by the steam and afterwards condensed, and form what is called the distillate. It is altogether a mistake to imagine that the ordinary spirits of commerce are represented by their equivalent of pure alcohol. We are much astonished to find in the ordinary analysis of beer, wine, brandy, whisky, gin, and rum, and indeed of any other spirits subjected to the usual examination, that it is considered sufficient to state that they contain a certain amount of alcohol in proportion to the water, and to give the amount of the solid ingredients, either in solution or suspension.

Such an analysis conveys an incorrect notion of the true constituents, for we have to take into account the number of other fluids, the influence of which must inevitably modify, to a greater or less degree, all the effects producible, either by fermented beverages or spirituous liquids in which they are contained.

We have to notice, particularly, the aldehydes, which distil at very low temperatures, not exceeding 87° Fahrenheit; the ethers, which, together with the aldehydes, contain all the finer and more volatile flavours, as well as the more subtle of the aromas peculiar to the products of fermentation; and the whole range of entirely volatile substances which accompany both these compounds, the boiling point of which does not exceed 100° Fahrenheit. With very little of the ordinary effects of alcohol, all these are so extremely diffusible, that the stimulus they create of themselves

Spirits. 119

cannot be measured by any comparison with that of pure alcohol.

We are tolerably well acquainted with the action of some of these ethers. Restorative medicine would lose some of its most important agents, if the ethers were expunged from the pharmacopeia. Yet these are almost universally estimated in conjunction with the true alcohol in spirits (ethyl alcohol); not only so, but with those other alcohols of a much higher boiling point, which contain certain odoriferous principles in close association with other poisonous matters, and which in a conglomerate form are denominated fusel oil (amylic alcohols).

All this may appear complicated, but it is, unfortunately, the nature of the distillates which we recognise as ordinary spirits of commerce. Unless we understand the different constituents which are to be found in these compounds, we might as well revert to the old standard test for the value of spirituous liquors, by the hydrometer, which merely gives the specific gravity of any number of compounds that may be present, or perhaps we should have to remain satisfied with the still more valuable experience (?) which is afforded of the purity and suitability of these liquors by the effects the next morning after partaking of them.

We have assigned to the aldehydes and ethers a

special diffusibility as well as delicacy of flavour and scent which is peculiar to them. We have not hesitated to class the generality of these among the remedies which are to be most highly esteemed among stimulants. Their medicinal use by themselves, however, must be regulated by the most competent advice. Here, we have to regard them in their relative position in connection with alcohol.

The ordinary distillates from fermented liquors contain only a moderate amount of the lighter ethereal products, until the spirit has been kept for some time, or has been subjected to a very special process of distillation. In either case, the proportion of volatile matters boiling at lower temperatures is found to be greatly increased, and this process is attended by the production of a distinctive perfume, and flavour.

It is not necessary to enter upon the minutiæ of this most complex subject, nor to attempt to define to what extent some of these may be due to the heavier aromatic constituents. We must, however, draw attention to the fact that pure alcohol contains very little, if any, of these. Indeed, in proportion to its purity, there is a corresponding loss of scent and taste, and excepting the sensation of heat, which it occasions on the palate, pure alcohol has no distinctive amount of either of these peculiarities. Pure alcohol boils

Spirits.

at a temperature of 173°, and can only be obtained by distillation after mixing with half its weight of fresh quicklime. Absolute alcohol, such as is thereby attained, has a specific gravity of ·973, and may be regarded as ether and a certain percentage of water, which cannot be removed without decomposing the alcohol.

Proof spirit consists, as nearly as may be, of equal parts of absolute alcohol and water; and in consequence of proof spirit being taken as the standard of alcoholic strength in all fluids by the Excise, great discrepancies may be observed in the manner of reporting the analysis of various fermented and spirituous liquors. Some chemists adhere to the per-centage of absolute alcohol which they contain, others adopt the proof spirit; while in many of the tables constructed a few years back, and which we are sorry to find copied into most of the later works upon the subject; alcoholic strengths of various beverages have been estimated by the highest standard of the then pharmacopeia, which had a specific gravity of ·825, and contained about ten per cent. of water. Brand's tables were all reckoned according to this latter standard, and others have used the alcoholic tables of Drinkwater, Ure, Fownes, and Tralles. Those of the Excise Department are not in accordance with any except Ure's, and are in themselves by no means accurate. Many of the divergencies may be accounted for by the use of these different tables, but quite as many must be undoubtedly due to the attempt at estimation by mere specific gravity of the various alcohols and ethers which come over in the distillate together, but which, in reality, if fractionated, are found to possess different specific gravities and different boiling points.

Before entering upon the characteristics of the various spirits in ordinary use, it may be well to describe as shortly as possible the general process of distillation. Any fermented liquor being taken and heated in a close vessel or still, the lighter portions of the volatile matters are first converted into vapour. If a pipe or head connect the still with the worm or other condensing apparatus, surrounded with a cool medium such as water or ice, these vapours will be again condensed and separated from those fluids which have not yet attained their boiling points. Although they are roughly separated, they carry over a certain portion of the vapours of the alcohols left in the still, which would not otherwise be enabled to rise over the head. They are, therefore, always mixed with a considerable quantity of vapours of alcohol, and water, and other liquids of higher boiling points.

As the heat increases, the alcohol is itself vaporised, and, as it expands so as to fill the condensing tube, is cooled to such a degree that it again becomes liquid. With this, as in the former instance, a considerable quantity of water is carried over, and the evolution of spirit of varying alcoholicity is not completed until the temperature of 212° has been reached.

According to the amount of spirit in the original fermented liquor, the distillate will be weaker or stronger, but it requires to be redistilled or rectified before it will attain the strength desired, and without which it is impossible to get rid of the large amount of fusel oil and other noxious products which the first distillation of fermented liquors almost invariably contains.

We need not describe the ingenious methods by which continuous distillation and rectification can be achieved, nor will time or space permit an adequate exemplification of the marvellous advantage to be obtained from a thorough, effective, and scientific rectification. But we shall have to allude to this point more particularly in connection with whisky. It is enough to say that the small still system can only produce drinkable spirits at one operation, when the foreshot or first portion which comes over is removed, and when of the remainder only a certain portion is taken for drinking purposes; that which is left is termed feints, from the unpleasant character of its smell and taste.

In the ordinary way, spirit is distilled in Great Britain from grain and malt, the commoner qualities having their mash consisting mainly of raw grain, with just sufficient malt introduced to gradually convert the rest. In the economy of malt, the conversion of the raw grain is insufficiently carried out, and in distilling the extract in solution an amount of amylic alcohol (fusel oil) is contemporaneously evolved with the true and purer spirit.

In Scotland, many distilleries use malt only, or malt with so moderate a proportion of grain that no more fusel oil is carried over than must necessarily occur in all raw distillations. It is then the work of the rectifier, who may in some instances be also the distiller, to remove as much as he can of these deleterious matters, without sacrificing the higher flavours which convey the distinctive peculiarities of whisky.

Some persons have imagined that whisky is composed of spirit, into which other flavouring matters have been imported, and we are afraid that a large amount of the cheaper descriptions of spirits sold under this denomination are so compounded. Spirit the most impure and objectionable is largely imported from Holland, Germany, and France, also from Russia (rye spirit), which is rendered as free as possible from its own nauseous peculiarities;

Spirits.

beet-root spirit, potato spirit, and spirit distilled from rice and every description of damaged grain, are imported to this country in enormous quantities, and at prices with which our own distillers cannot compete, and, therefore, offer great temptation to unprincipled rectifiers; and, when we are assured that such spirit is offered at prices varying from 10d. to 1s. 4d. per gallon, we can easily understand how such large quantities of vile and deleterious spirits are compounded from these noxious bases.

The rectification of these spirits demands the use of large quantities of grey salts, which are composed of caustic lime and potash. By this means what is termed silent spirit is produced, bearing no resemblance whatever to the pure distillate of whisky spirit. No one could be found to drink this silent spirit, unless he had proclivities akin to those savages who luxuriate in such delicacies as train oil and whale blubber. For common consumption, therefore, the silent spirit requires flavouring, whether it be made into whisky, gin, or brandy.

But it is necessary first to follow out the production of true whisky, inasmuch as this alone of all spirits distilled in this country should be the most direct product of the distillation of malted grain.

If, in the first place, a fine malt spirit is produced,

and this is rectified by continuous distillation to the required strength, it must then be stored for several years before it can be considered wholesome or fit to drink. Some whiskies mature with much greater rapidity than others, but this depends mainly upon the amount of fusel oil which they contain. In almost every instance new whiskies are imbued with these dangerous constituents to a degree which renders them highly injurious and sometimes poisonous, and, as it is difficult to obtain any guarantee that all the different whiskies which are blended together in the ordinary whiskies of commerce have attained a sufficient age to reduce the amount of fusel oil to its minimum, the public will do well to assure themselves that they are not purchasing blends of whisky which contain varying proportions of unmatured spirit.

From a large number of samples of whisky which we have examined during the past year, we conclude that there are not many brands of aged whisky which can be depended upon in this particular, and we have therefore been gratified in having proved to our own satisfaction that a novel process of distillation* which has been adopted in Scotland does eliminate to a most perfect degree the fusel oil, which would otherwise be only got rid of by the lapse of years.

* Bernard's.

Spirits.

Gin is invariably compounded from silent spirit, or the portion of spirit which remains after the finer whisky spirit has been drawn off. This is treated in the same manner as the foreign spirits before mentioned; and at this after-rectification, are added the various flavourings of the different gin spinners.

The best gin is flavoured with juniper berries, angelica root, coriander seeds, and a few other matters which give it a characteristic flavour. Other compounders use turpentine, capsicum, and ingredients, which convey the notion of far greater strength, after dilution, than would be given by the amount of alcohol which the gin contains.

But, in any case, gin must be regarded as a flavoured and medicated spirit, which, although to a certain extent admissible in some instances, when largely diluted with water, still, from the circumstance that it is usually taken without any further dilution than that to which it is submitted at the hands of the retailer, is probably more injurious in its effects upon the body than any other spirit.

Brandy should be the pure distillate of wine, but we fear that very little brandy of that character comes into this country. We are aware that large quantities of damaged wine are distilled, but the great use of the spirit so obtained is that of fortifying other wines. In the brandy districts it is true that grapes are pressed, and the wine so made is distilled. But with the great majority of instances the merks or marks, which are technical terms for the residue of the wine-pressing, are fermented and distilled, furnishing no inconsiderable proportion of the brandy which we import.

In addition to the spirit so obtained, an enormous quantity of grain spirit is turned into brandy by flavouring with the so-called oil of cognac and other essences which give it that which is now generally held to be the true brandy flavour; and when we find that the very characteristic which may be regarded as of medicinal value, namely, its astringency, and which, together with its colour, can only be acquired from the oaken casks in which it is stored, or from certain added matters, it must be seen that brandy owes most of its peculiarities to adventitious aids.

It is on this account that ordinary brandy spirit produces a train of symptoms so clearly marked in persons who drink it habitually. A pure brandy, distilled alone from a good white wine, should possess neither colour nor astringency, and we may remark that no pure spirit as it comes from the still either contains or will develop any colour whatever, unless it is brought into contact with colouring matters which it can absorb.

Rum is distilled from sugar, and as the generality of it is made from molasses, a large quantity of peculiar ethers and alcohols are carried over into the distillate, which are seldom found in any other kind of spirit. One of these is butyl alcohol, which, as it becomes oxidised, produces certain volatile flavours, identical with those evolved during the decomposition of butter and cheese.

To the presence of these compounds must be attributed that condition of so-called biliousness following the drinking of rum which has not been kept for a sufficient length of time. When rum has been stored for very many years, butyric ether is formed, which gives to it the true pineapple flavour. This is, unfortunately, however, but too easily simulated, and, therefore, affords no criterion of that thoroughly matured spirit we can consider wholesome.

Having now described the principal varieties of fermented and distilled alcoholic beverages generally consumed, it is, perhaps, of even greater importance to describe their effects, both as stimulants and dietetics. In the perennial discussion of this subject, which has lately acquired a greater interest than ever, the general view taken is supposed to relate to one particular alcohol. The innumerable modifications produced by its combination with many kinds of extractives, its presence in varying proportions as affecting its immediate influence, and the train of consequences following the systematic use of any of them, appear to have been altogether overlooked.

Of the eleven alcohols, each having a definite and different elementary composition, only five, or at the outside six, have any immediate connection with the alcoholic stimulants of common use. What is usually understood by alcohol is that which is denominated ethylic, and is best understood under the term pure spirits of wine; but as an adulterant, methylic alcohol (wood spirit) has sometimes been attempted to be mixed in with the commoner spirits of commerce, after a sufficient rectification to remove the greater part of its distinctive odour and flavour; a much lower duty being charged on the manufacture of wood spirit than that of spirits of wine for consumption.

For this purpose, that which is called methylated spirits is mixed to contain ten per cent. of the former, for the purpose of dissolving certain gums in the manufacture of varnish. In the attempt to evade the duty which would be levied upon drinkable spirit, this methylated spirit is subjected to different processes of rectification, with the idea of removing the methyl alcohol. But as the entire removal of this methyl alcohol would be attained with so great an expense, that it would be rendered unprofitable, it is usually only partially performed, the result being a spirit containing an appreciable quantity of this most objectionable contamination.

This is a comparatively rare form of adulteration, but certain samples have been submitted for examination which contain a sufficient quantity of crude wood spirit to render them injurious, although by ingenious means the obnoxious flavour and smell inherent to commercial methylated spirit have been almost entirely covered, if not removed.

The next alcohol is propylic, which is naturally present to a small extent in the distillates of the mark brandies of the South of France; it produces a slight acidity in its oxidation by age, and however much we may deprecate the use of spirits containing this alcohol, a slight flavouring of it is not always objected to by drinkers of coarse spirits.

Butylic alcohol has been already mentioned as a constituent of rum, and some wines develop flavours not altogether dissimilar to those of rum, when long keeping has oxidised certain portions of their compounds.

Amylic alcohol, of which fusel oil is mainly composed, furnishes considerations of much greater importance than any of the foregoing in their relation to the spirits of commerce. It has been regarded, but without any foundation, as an adulterant; that is to say, as something which has been added for flavouring or for fraudulently increasing the bulk of British spirits; it is, however, a constant product of almost every kind of distillation.

The spirit of pure fermented sugar is free from any amylic alcohol. The next purest source of alcoholic fermentation is that of pure grape juice which is fully fermented out. Almost equal to this, is the alcohol developed by the fermentation of perfectly malted barley, such as exists in the best samples of beer and whisky. Whenever the fermentation of raw grain is carried out with the assistance of only a small quantity of malted grain, a considerable quantity of amylic alcohol is formed from the decomposition of the starch which has not been changed into sugar, and from this circumstance the name amylic alcohol has been derived from the word amylum, starch.

The vilest description of amylic alcohol, which carries with it the most disgusting volatile matters accompanying fusel oil, is found when damaged grain, rice, potatoes, or beetroot form the distiller's mash; and incredible quantities of crude spirit containing these abominations are shipped to different ports of this country for rectification, and are here blended with all kinds of wines, and mixed with other spirits and flavourings.

There are certain combinations of the higher alcohols which accompany the distillates of all mashes made from coarse damaged vegetable substance; but these are, perhaps, more prevalent in the distillation of the commoner brandies of the wine-producing countries than in that of raw grain. The crudity of these common brandies is due to the carelessness of preparation, and hence the deleterious properties justly attributed to them.

Premising that a distinctive action must be occasioned by each of the several alcohols enumerated above, and that these vary also according to the proportion present, the immediate effects of beverages containing ethylic or common alcohol must now be pointed out. In doing so, it is necessary to mention two distinct classes of effects, which in all cases vary with the alcoholic strength of the fluids imbibed; first, those produced upon the membranes with which these fluids come into contact; secondly, those produced upon the nervous and circulatory systems, and through them upon those tissues in which the more minute vessels are distributed.

The specific action of alcohol on the membranes depends upon its strength. In its concentrated form it acts as an astringent, by causing contraction of fibre through the abstraction of water from it. This is proved in the laboratory by the preservative action that it exercises in not permitting a sufficient quantity to exist in the muscular or other tissues to enable them to putrefy.

As soon as the alcohol becomes diluted with water beyond a certain point, this preservative action is lost, and its power of causing contraction in living membrane is also reduced by the amount of its dilution. So that, in considering what are termed the effects of alcohol, it is of the utmost importance that the actual alcoholic strength of the beverage spoken of should be known. As the tendency of alcohol, even moderately diluted, is to become still more so, the effect upon living membrane must be always less and less astringent, and the sensation of heat upon the tongue and palate, felt in drinking strong alcoholic beverages, is undoubtedly due to astringency.

The phenomena next in sequence are the effects of alcoholic fluids upon the secretions of the stomach and bowels. The active principles of those important solvents of food, termed the gastric, pancreatic, and salivary juices, are always precipitated and rendered inert whenever alcoholic fluids are taken beyond a certain strength; but it must be remembered that when these alcoholic fluids reach the stomach in very small quantities, the alcohol is generally absorbed with great rapidity, and in many nstances the increased flow of gastric juice and other fluids, caused through the agency of the stimulus applied to the nervous system by its absorption, more than compensates for the temporary arrest of the digestive power of these juices.

The effects of the constant taking of strong alcoholic fluids upon the liver must also be recognised. It is unnecessary to describe at length the complex structure of this organ; but from its close vascular connection with the stomach, it will be readily understood that a large quantity of the alcohol taken into it finds its way directly through the circulation into the liver. When this habitually occurs, the first effect noticeable is a condition of congestion, which interferes with the activity of the biliary excretions and the elimination of bilious matters from the blood; this is followed by an inflammatory condition resulting in interstitial deposit and the enlargement which necessarily accompanies this condition, which is afterwards changed into one of contraction caused by the reabsorption of this deposited matter.

In this stage of disease, that which is generally known by the name of obstruction occurs. The healthy circulation of the blood through the liver is retarded to an extent which seriously interferes with the action of the heart; and the kidneys having to eliminate a certain portion of the bile, which under healthy conditions is never present in their secretion, frequently become themselves diseased. Thus, various forms of dropsy, from their more prominent symptoms termed hepatic, cardiac, or renal, manifest themselves.

Passing on to the effects of alcohol upon the nervous and circulatory systems, undoubtedly the first action is that which is generally understood by the word "stimulation;" and if this condition be not prolonged or too frequently repeated, it may be looked upon as beneficial; but where alcoholic beverages are taken in large quantities or too frequently, the condition of depression following this exhilaration is such as to render a further supply of these beverages a too welcome alleviation. Under these circumstances, a certain per-centage of alcohol is maintained in the circulation, which produces a well-marked train of effects upon all the tissues of the body.

Among these, the febrile conditions are greatly aggravated by the amylic and other alcohols which may be present, and which can only be regarded as deleterious impurities. The action of fusel oil upon the brain, apart from the injurious effects on the stomach which it produces, is so irritating as to cause symptoms closely allied to the delirium of fever.

On this account we cannot lay too great stress upon the necessity of abstaining from any spirits which contain it. It may be generally accepted that the per-centage of proof spirit, whether contained in wine or taken as spirits and water, should never exceed 30 per cent.

In dealing with modifications of alcoholic beverages, which arise from their combination with extractive matters, we have endeavoured to explain that the presence of a moderate amount of saccharine is of less moment when the spirituous strength is low, such, for instance, as is to be found in beer or certain descriptions of wine; and when we consider the question of liqueurs, we find that many of these are little better than highly alcoholised syrups heavily flavoured. If these flavourings consist of volatile ethers and essences, little objection can be raised to them.

But in the case of the ordinary bitters of commerce, when their flavours are derived from extractives and alkaloids which are cumulative in their effects, dissolved in strong alcohol frequently of the worst description, a strong syrup enables it to be drunk without diluting the powerful bitters which cover the coarse flavour of the spirit. All combine to render such compounds unwholesome in the extreme.

A light liqueur of agreeable flavour and moderate alcoholicity, in which the spirit is of the required purity, would no doubt be generally accepted as free from these defects. If to this be added a delicate diffusible tonic and a comparatively small proportion of saccharine, such a liqueur would be found really beneficial as an occasional tonic stimulant, and might be said to be superior to the majority of wines which are generally taken for these purposes.

CHAPTER X.

TEA, COFFEE, COCOA.

OF these non-alcoholic stimulants, tea obtains an importance in this country, far exceeding the consumption of either of the others. This is evidenced by the largeness of the ever-increasing imports. The relative value of different kinds of tea is still, however, but little understood. In the purchase of certain descriptions, as compared with others, strength of flavour is more sought for than true delicacy, indeed, roughness is supposed to co-exist in the same degree with its refreshing qualities.

Too little heed has been paid to the amount of extract which can be obtained from its infusion, and too much value is attached to what is deemed pungency, and the depth of colour which is imparted to the water. As long as tea-dealers can sell a low-priced tea which has sufficient bitterness, blackness, and astringency to make a strong impression upon the palate, such tea is considered cheap and particularly suited to the requirements of those who wish to get the most they can for their money.

When tea of a better description is desired, advantage is taken of the prompting of a more educated taste to increase the nominal value to an extent which precludes the general consumption of the finer kinds. If we consider the composition of tea, we find that the diffusible alkaloid "thein," to which its stimulating effects are chiefly due, may exist in an inverse ratio both with price and flavour.

The amount of astringency may also exceed or fall short of that which would be considered most desirable, while the amount of tea flavour which can be obtained from a given weight of different samples of tea is so little understood by even professional tea-tasters, that true economy in buying is often neglected in the endeavour to supply an article possessing the rugged characteristics before pointed out.

The adulteration of tea, to which public attention has been largely directed during the last few years, is one on which extremely crude notions are prevalent. Prosecutions have taken place when a few grains of sand have been found, which really constitute no palpable fraud upon the purchaser. Grave objections have also been taken to the facing of tea by the Chinese, which, by the way, is only done in compliance with the desire of the English retailer; and the matters, so introduced, have been greatly exaggerated, both with regard to the proportion they bear to the leaves, and also as to the injurious influences they are supposed to possess.

We are altogether averse to the entire system of tea-facing and colouring, more, however, on the ground that it tends to pass off an inferior tea for a better article, than in consequence of any great injury which is likely to be caused by it.

We have been far more concerned in the endeavour to obtain a reliable standard by which the real value of different samples of tea may be estimated, and we are happy to be able, at length, to place reliance upon the recently formulated means of making what is called a tea "assay." This method of analysis determines the amount of extract obtained by infusion, the proportion of astringency, the stimulating component, and the entire quantity of the mineral matters.

By this means the presence of even two or three per cent. of exhausted tea leaves can be detected without fail. Any addition of colouring matter, or, in fact, any other adulteration, is immediately revealed; and we are convinced, that by adopting a scientific examination of the constituents, in contradistinction to the empyrical method adopted by tea-tasters, the public will be able to judge for themselves whether, in satisfying their palates, they are purchasing that which represents the best money value; besides which, some security is afforded to the merchant in the purchase of the cargoes.

Coffee also contains a corresponding alkaloid, which has been termed cafein; but the chief difference between coffee and tea consists in the fatty matters and in the volatile oils. As much as ten or twelve per cent. of fat is present in the coffee-bean. There is also a considerable amount of sugar and dextrine.

It is difficult to compare the per-centage composition of coffee with tea, in estimating the effects produced by drinking a cup of one or the other, according to taste. A much greater weight of coffee is generally used than that of tea in preparing the same quantity of beverage for breakfast or other meals, the greater astringency of tea rendering it more economical in this respect.

Unlike tea, which is used without any further treatment after it is imported, the quality of coffee depends, to a great extent, upon the care which is exercised in the roasting. Not only so, it must be freshly roasted and ground fine, the degree of fineness of the grinding having much to do with the amount of extract obtainable by percolation.

It is altogether beyond our present scope to consider the different varieties of coffee, from the veritable Mocha to the lowest colonial. In France, the selection of beans has far more to do with the excellence of the beverage than its domestic preparation. In that country all the beans are most carefully hand-picked, to exclude with the utmost rigour any that are defective or damaged.

The presence of a very few mouldy beans, or those which have become decomposed, is sufficient to injure a large quantity of the very finest sample; and if a proper system of percolation is adopted, by which the infusion first obtained is returned and strained through the partially exhausted ground coffee (of which an adequate quantity must not be stinted), as good a cup of coffee can be prepared in this country, from properly selected beans, fresh roasted and ground, as any that has ever delighted the epicure of Paris.

Little advance has been made in the improvement of the quality of coffee generally sold, but in the article of cocoa most noteworthy progress can be recorded, not, perhaps, so much in the amount of the importation of this article, as in its mechanical preparation.

Combining, as it does, an alkaloid with a considerable amount of nitrogenous matter, together with starch and gum, cocoa contains so large an amount of fatty matter, that its mere infusion is incapable of extracting those properties which would enable it to compete with tea or coffee.

By bruising the cocoa nib, and simmering it for many hours, a certain amount of flavour is obtained, and this partakes, to some extent, of the refreshing character of tea; still, however, this is so extravagant a method of obtaining, at best, a poor result, that it has been found necessary to grind the nib after roasting, and drink it rather as a mixture than an infusion. The first attempts that were made in this direction partially failed, in consequence of the difficulty of taking up the large amount of fat, equal to nearly half of its bulk.

The ingenuity of the dealers was next exemplified by their causing it to assume the form of an emulsion, by adding considerable quantities of starch or farina. When boiling water is poured upon the ground cocoa mixed with any kind of starch, the thickening so well known to every laundress takes place, the particles of cocoa fat included are held in suspension by the coagulum formed by starch, and a mixture of greater or less consistency is obtained, according to the quantity used.

Unfortunately, such preparations of cocoa resemble too closely the composition of melted butter. There can be no doubt that the opportunity afforded to manufacturers of lowering the price of cocoa, which realizes more than a shilling per pound wholesale, by the addition of farina at 2½d., has tended to disgust that portion of the community who object to mixtures, such as these, in lieu of the fragrant, refreshing qualities of true cocoa.

Within a short period, several manufacturers have overcome this difficulty by removing a large portion of the superfluous fat; they are thus able to grind cocoa to the highest degree of fineness, so that, in fact, it can be mixed with boiling water without the necessity of any extraneous matter to hold it in suspension.

This removal of the excess fat also renders the cocoa extremely easy of digestion; and when so prepared, it can be recommended as affording one of the best descriptions of nutritive beverages adapted to the requirements of the most delicate stomachs.

Of those who could not tolerate the thick greasy mixtures which have been so persistently puffed under the name of homœopathic cocoas and other catching titles, few are found to object to those more scientifically prepared cocoas which have been just described; and as the question of pure versus adulterated cocoas was discussed with no little acrimony a short time back, we are enabled to speak positively to the perfect purity and highly desirable qualities of some of the many samples which have been recently submitted to the most searching investigation.*

Tea and coffee contain but a low per-centage of ingredients capable of assimilation, or conversion into bodily tissue; they may, therefore, rank chiefly as stimulants in the effects they produce upon the nervous system; and, as with alcoholic fluids, so in the case of these non-alcoholic stimulants, due moderation must be observed, or the effects of over-indulgence will be evidenced by a condition of nervous irritability and consequent depression similar to that which follows the excessive use of alcohol.

Cocoa, when deprived of superabundant fat, retains much of the stimulating effects attributed both to coffee and tea. It has, however, in addition the nutritive value of the nitrogenous matter which it possesses to a far greater extent than either tea or coffee. On this ground it has a real food value; and when the question of dietetic economy has to be considered, it must be acknowledged that cocoa has a higher value than either of them.

* Cadbury's Cocoa Essence and Schweitzer's Cocoatina are prominent examples of the success attending the sale of scientifically prepared pure cocoas, even from a time prior to the Adulteration of Foods Act.

CHAPTER XI.

KITCHEN ILLUSTRATIONS AND COOKERY.

THIS subject comprises no small portion of domestic economy. If the various articles of food are well bought, properly prepared for cooking, and then judiciously subjected to such culinary operations as are best adapted to develop their nutriment and agreeable flavours to the fullest extent, most food must be generally considered wholesome.

If veal and pork are less easy of digestion than beef or mutton, and if some vegetables are prone to disagree with a certain number of persons, it must be remembered that the existing condition of the digestive process may be estimated by the activity with which they perform their functions indiscriminately upon all articles of food.

If sufficient exercise is taken, and a healthy appetite is not immoderately indulged, good cookery will aid previous selection as to quality, and, as we know, the less eligible descriptions of food may be taken, not only with impunity, but with considerable satisfaction.

As, however, we should have but very little to say if we were to address alone those to whom nothing comes amiss, we must endeavour to afford assistance, both in the selection of food and its cooking, to enable persons with less sturdy powers of digestion to enjoy and assimilate a sufficient variety of the different kinds of food. We are anxious also to relieve as far as possible the monotony which often ensues from depending too exclusively upon the superior digestibility of a few viands which are generally supposed to be more suitable in such cases.

It is obviously impossible to give instruction on what the cookery books entitle "how to market." But until a little more care is devoted to cookery, our knowledge of how to purchase, both economically and with some judgment as to quality, is valueless, and we may still pursue the haphazard plan of allowing tradespeople to send in pretty much what they please, in contradistinction to the care and vigilance which is exercised with so much advantage in the cities of France and Germany.

We have in England much to contend against, in the indisposition butchers and other tradesmen manifest to supply the small quantities which enable a sufficient diversity to be given to the continental breakfast and dinner. There is, happily, no such thing as cold meat cookery abroad, nor, indeed, is it usual to serve up cooked food a second time, or after it has become cold.

Here, if two or three persons wish to partake of anything beyond chops or steaks, they must be content to see what is left of the leg of mutton or joint of beef reproduced on several occasions. As, however, we have to deal with our opportunities, such as they are, and not with such as we ought to have, we can only inculcate the necessity for exercising all possible ingenuity in avoiding the constant recurrence of some of our standard dishes, which, particularly in the article of meat, may be said to contrast the alternatives of beef for mutton, by suggesting that of mutton for beef.

If we take as an example of want of thrift in the purchase of meat, the way in which a few mutton chops are bought, this will give as good an instance, perhaps, as if we could enter upon similar details attending the other dealings with the butcher.

We note that if a loin of mutton is taken down from the hooks, the number of chops wished for are cut off, and they are then weighed, a few scraps having been previously removed from the ends. After weighing, however, the butcher proceeds to trim them somewhat more closely; and, in a general way, a difference of several ounces in the pound will be discovered between the weight charged for and that obtained.

Now, if the cook were to again remove a considerable portion of the remaining fat, almost invariably in excess of that which is ever eaten, this fat might be carefully rendered down, and made available for other purposes, without any loss. But if the chop is to be cooked, as alone it can be, to preserve the juice of the meat, and develop that peculiarity of flavour which a well-cooked mutton chop is supposed to possess, the operation of broiling over a sufficiently rapid fire converts a large portion of the fat into fuel, a result which demonstrates the cost and waste attending so simple a mode of cooking as that of broiling.

A half-pound mutton chop when cut from the cascase rarely weighs more than five ounces by the time it is brought to table, and of this the bone and portion of the tail, which are frequently left, still further reduce the amount of nutriment so obtained to little more than two or three ounces.

By the ordinary methods of boiling much food value is extracted; hence the value of the broth. But we are afraid, from various experiences, that the greater part of what is termed pot liquor is usually thrown away, or otherwise badly utilised.

To understand how this is likely to occur, we must endeavour to explain the action of heat upon different kinds of food; and, from the variety of methods in which it is applied, it will be shown t act as a means of extraction in certain instances, while in others it enables the extractive matters to be retained and preserved within the food itself.

The three principal modes of applying heat to food are those of roasting, boiling, and stewing, which, in other words, may be expressed as subjecting the various matters to dry heat and moist heat, with modifications of temperature. The operation of roasting, taking meat as an example, consists in submitting it to the immediate action of dry heat, whether directly from an open fire, radiated, or reflected.

It differs essentially from that of baking, not only in temperature, but also in the amount of ventilation, or constant accession of fresh air, which removes from the meat all the unpleasant emanations which it would be liable to reabsorb in a close oven; this is attended by a considerable amount of loss, both of value and of juice by evaporation. But no other method of cooking can impart that most agreeable and delicate flavour, which is designated osmazome, to the same perfection that can be obtained by roasting, and this cannot be obtained in any close oven, however ingenious the arrangement of some kitcheners may be.

Of these there are an infinite variety, and in some of them an attempt has been made to secure ventilation, which reduces the objection that has been previously taken to this modification of baking.

The most successful of these, that has come before our notice, is one in which the heat is communicated by means of gas burners, which are so arranged that they secure perfect combustion, and force a large current of hot-air throughout every portion of the roaster, and this combines so great an economy of heat with excellence of ventilation, that one of the smallest ordinary fish-tail burners, placed in a properly constructed chimney, suffices to roast a 7lb. joint at the cost of less than a halfpenny for the gas consumed.*

The temperature best adapted for roasting varies from 400 to 500 degrees Fahrenheit. Contrary to the ordinary practice, meat should be subjected to the greatest heat for the first quarter of an hour, after which it should be reduced by about 100 degrees either by removing the joint farther from the fire or lowering the amount of gas.

As an instance of this, the most perfect method of broiling is that of dipping a chop or steak into a little oil or melted fat, by which means, when placed on the gridiron, it immediately blazes up, scorching, and instantaneously sealing the mouths of the tubules of the meat. This action is so instantaneous, that it is entirely superficial, and

* Southby's patent.

leaves the interior of the meat to be gradually though quickly cooked at a more moderate temperature. To preserve evenness in broiling, the meat requires to be constantly turned with tongs, and on no account ought a fork to be used, since by puncturing the meat its juices are lost.

Baking is only adapted for cooking where the application of heat is required to be sustained at a lower temperature than that of roasting, and where no objection can be taken to the presence of a certain amount of vapour. Although this is incompatible with the crispness of roast meat, it is, no doubt, advantageous to pastry, which would otherwise be dried up on the surface before the interior could be sufficiently cooked.

Boiling, which is the application of moist heat, and which, in no instance, can exceed 212°, renders this mode inapplicable when a lower temperature is desired, in which case the more accurate term would be stewing or simmering.

For the same reason that we have advocated the application of the higher temperatures for roasting at the commencement, so we, also, in the case of boiling meat, where the pot liquor is not intended to be used for soup, cannot too strongly urge the necessity for plunging the meat into boiling water for a few minutes before the actual cooking commences. After this has been done, the vessel must be withdrawn from the fire for some minutes to allow the water to become cooler, never again bringing it up to the full boiling point.

The reason for this is to prevent the juice of the meat from being gradually dissolved out and taken up by the water. The convenience of such procedure is shown conversely in the process of making soup, and is of course available to a certain extent when the meat is intended to be eaten, and the broth is afterwards made into soup.

Having insisted upon the necessity of meat being only subjected to the boiling temperature at the commencement of the process, we have to point out that this boiling temperature must be maintained for the proper cooking of all kinds of puddings made of suet for a period much longer than is generally supposed. If we assume that it is advisable to double the length of time suggested by the most *exigeants* writers on cookery, we hope we shall not make too great a demand on the patience of the cooks.

Similarly, we have always found recipes for cooking farinaceous foods direct far too short a time for their cookery, and they are further not sufficiently particular as to temperature, the essential point in the proper cooking of these foods being the proper swelling up of the starch corpuscles throughout the whole, and at the same time coagulating the albuminoid matter without rendering the gluten tough and stringy. This is best attained by prolonging the period of their cookery, and reducing the temperature to about 180°.

The cooking of vegetables in some instances depends upon the care which is exercised in extracting certain unpleasant and coarse flavours. This is well exemplified in the case of cabbage and onions. It may be observed that the latter can only be rendered wholesome by frequently changing the water in which they have been boiled, and that even garlic may be rendered so mild and free from acridity by carrying this out to the fullest extent, that while it can be recognised as a delicious adjunct to many dishes, hardly any one unacquainted with the continental method of cooking it would be aware of its presence.

On the other hand, the vast majority of the vegetables usually boiled would better preserve their nutritive value if they were steamed; their own peculiar flavours are preserved by this means; and although some have objected to a certain loss of brightness in colour, many of the most delicate vegetables can only be thoroughly appreciated when cooked by steam.

CHAPTER XII.

HAVING touched upon the main points of importance in connection with the commoner articles of food, we feel how inadequate any attempt must be to do more than excite a certain interest in the endeavour to convey even the most general information on so large a subject.

In order to arrive at a really accurate knowledge of the composition of food as it relates to the nutrition of the body, and also in the very important aspect it assumes in pleasing the palate, both by variety and judicious selection, a greater knowledge of physiology, of chemistry, and even of botany would be required, than is generally comprised in the ordinary course of education.

It may seem a simple matter for each to decide for himself that which he likes, and therefore fancies is best adapted for him. But without more accurate data, and more widely extended experience of the effects of the various kinds of food than can ever fall to the lot of one individual whose observation is restricted to his own person, the result must be unsatisfactory.

In the present day, when no sufficient censorship exists to expose the unblushing falsehoods put forth by advertisers of all sorts of food, both liquid and solid, which are, in reality, anything but what they pretend to be, it becomes necessary to obtain some better insight into the general principles which govern this subject than the vague notions generally entertained.

When it is popularly supposed that the thicker the soup, the more nutritious it must be; when the most marvellous virtues are attributed to calves'-foot jelly, arrowroot, and corn-flour; and when port wine is regarded as infusing, by some mysterious means, vital power and muscular strength into the most enfeebled frames, it is necessary that the composition of these articles, and their effects, should be made known.

It is absolutely necessary for every one to comprehend that, unless tissue-forming principles are taken into the body, tissue cannot be maintained and reproduced. In fact, that unless matter capable of distribution and assimilation is conveyed by means of food, inevitable waste must occur, and all the powers and functions of life become impaired.

In other words, starvation ensues, not only when

there is an insufficient quantity of food consumed in the aggregate, but starvation of certain tissues takes place whenever there is a lack of the peculiar principles necessary for their support.

This is the case in health, and a well-regulated system of diet in the treatment of disease is of even higher importance than the drugs which have been found to be most useful in controlling its more prominent symptoms.

Diseases of an acute or active nature doubtless require the use of powerful drugs, and in these, nourishment must be given in forms as fluid and readily absorbable as possible; but in that very large class of diseases which may be described as constitutional, or chronic, no benefit can be looked for from the use of drugs, unless an intelligent supervision and rigid adherence to the rules of diet laid down be enforced.

As instances, we may mention those cases, unfortunately now so common, of gout, rheumatism, diabetes, etc., in all of which it can be proved most conclusively that more benefit is derived from proper diet and well-regulated habits of life than any special drugs which are known.

It is, we need hardly point out, fallacious in the extreme to imagine that occasional doses of medicine can successfully combat the results of daily and hourly indulgence in those very kinds of aliment which ought to be most carefully avoided. Nor can the effects of intemperance be remedied by any specific nostrums which can be devised.

If disordered or impaired bodily functions have already reduced the strength below its normal standard, this has only occurred from want of assimilation of food; it must be repaired from that source alone. The medicine in this case plays only the part of an auxiliary; the real work of rebuilding must be done by food.

THE END.

Printed by Hazell, Watson, and Viney, London and Aylesbury.

A SELECTION FROM

HENRY S. KING & CO.'S

LIST OF NEW BOOKS.

65, Cornhill, and 1, Paternoster Square.

May, 1876.

A SELECTION

FROM

HENRY S. KING AND CO.'S CATALOGUE.

NEW AND RECENTLY PUBLISHED WORKS.

CHILDREN'S BOOKS.

THREE SHILLINGS AND SIXPENCE EACH.

Works by the Author of "St. Olave's," "When I was a Little Girl," &c.

AUNT MARY'S BRAN PIE. Illustrated. Foolscap 8vo, cloth.

Sunnyland Stories. Illustrated. Foolscap 8vo, cloth.

Brave Men's Footsteps : a Book of Example and Anecdote for Young People. By the Editor of "Men who have Risen." With 4 Illustrations by C. Doyle. Third Edition. Crown 8vo cloth.

Pretty Lessons in Verse for Good Children, with some Lessons in Latin, in easy Rhyme. By SARA COLERIDGE. Illustrated. A New Edition. Foolscap 8vo, cloth.

Little Minnie's Troubles : an Every-Day Chronicle. By N. D'ANVERS. Illustrated by W. H. Hughes. Foolscap 8vo., cloth.

The Desert Pastor, Jean Jarousseau. By Colonel E. P. DE L'HOSTE. Translated from the French of Eugène Pelletan. With an Engraved Frontispiece. New Edition. Fcap. 8vo, cloth.

The Story of Our Father's Love, told to Children, being a New and Enlarged Edition of THEOLOGY FOR CHILDREN. By MARK EVANS. Foolscap 8vo, cloth.

Works by MARTHA FARQUHARSON.

Elsie Dinsmore. Illustrated, Foolscap 8vo, cloth.

Elsie's Girlhood. Illustrated, Foolscap 8vo, cloth.

Elsie's Holiday at Roselands. Illustrated, Fcap. 8vo, cloth.

The Little Wonder-Horn. A Second Series of "Stories told to a Child." By JEAN INGELOW. With Fifteen Illustrations. Square 24mo, cloth.

Plucky Fellows. A Book for Boys. By STEPHEN J. MACKENNA. With Six Illustrations. Second Edition. Crown 8vo, cloth.

The African Cruiser. A Midshipman's Adventures on the West Coast. By S. W. SADLER, R.N., Author of "Marshall Vavasour." A Book for Boys. With Three Illustrations. Third Edition. Crown 8vo, cloth.

Seeking His Fortune, and Other Stories. With 4 Illustrations. Crown 8vo, cloth.

Seven Autumn Leaves from Fairyland. Illustrated with Nine Etchings. Square 8vo, cloth.

Works by SARA COLERIDGE.

Pretty Lessons in Verse for Good Children, with some Lessons in Latin, in Easy Rhyme. A New Edition. Illustrated. Foolscap 8vo, cloth.

Phantasmion. A Fairy Romance. With an Introductory Preface by the Right Hon. Lord Coleridge of Ottery St. Mary. A New Edition. Illustrated. Crown 8vo, cloth, price 7s. 6d.

FIVE SHILLINGS EACH.

Works by JAMES BONWICK.

The Tasmanian Lily. With Frontispiece. Crown 8vo, cloth.

Mike Howe, the Bushranger of Van Diemen's Land.
With Frontispiece. Crown 8vo, cloth.

Rambles and Adventures of Our School Field Club:
its Adventures and Achievements. A Book for Boys. By G. C. DAVIES.
Crown 8vo, cloth.

Works by DAVID KER.

The Boy Slave in Bokhara: a Tale of Central Asia.
With Illustrations. Crown 8vo, cloth.

The Wild Horseman of the Pampas. Illustrated. Crown 8vo, cloth.

Fantastic Stories. By RICHARD LEANDER. Translated from the German by PAULINA B. GRANVILLE. With 8 Full-page Illustrations by M. E. Fraser-Tytler. Crown 8vo, cloth.

Her Title of Honour: a Book for Girls. By HOLME LEE.
New Edition, with Frontispiece. Crown 8vo, cloth.

At School with an Old Dragoon. By STEPHEN J. MACKENNA. With 6 Illustrations. Crown 8vo, cloth.

Slavonic Fairy Tales. From Russian, Servian, Polish, and Bohemian Sources. By JOHN T. NAAKÈ, of the British Museum. With 4 Illustrations. Crown 8vo, cloth.

Waking and Working; or, from Girlhood to Womanhood. By Mrs. G. S. REANEY. With Frontispiece. Crown 8vo, cloth.

Stories in Precious Stones. By HELEN ZIMMERN. With 6 Illustrations. Third Edition. Crown 8vo, cloth.

Works by Miss M. BETHAM-EDWARDS.

Kitty. With a Frontispiece. Crown 8vo, cloth, price 3s. 6d.

Mademoiselle Josephine's Fridays, and Other Stories.
Crown 8vo, cloth, price 7s. 6d.

By Still Waters. A Story for Quiet Hours. By EDWARD GARRETT. With Seven Illustrations. Crown 8vo, cloth, price 6s.

Works by Mrs. G. S. REANEY.

Waking and Working; or, from Girlhood to Womanhood. With a Frontispiece. Crown 8vo, cloth, price 5s.

Sunbeam Willie, and other Stories, for Home Reading and Cottage Meetings. 3 Illustrations. Small square, uniform with "Lost Gip," &c. Cloth, price 1s. 6d.

Locked Out: a Tale of the Strike. By ELLEN BARLEE. With a Frontispiece. Cloth, price 1s. 6d.

Daddy's Pet. A Sketch from Humble Life. By Mrs. ELLEN ROSS, ("Nelsie Brook.") With 6 Illustrations. Square crown 8vo. Uniform with "Lost Gip." Cloth, price 1s.

Works by the Author of "Jessica's First Prayer," (HESBA STRETTON).

The Wonderful Life. With Illustrated Frontispiece. Fcap. 8vo, cloth, price 2s. 6d. Ninth Thousand.

With Illustrations, square crown 8vo, cloth, price 1s. 6d. each.

The Crew of the Dolphin.

Cassy. Twenty-seventh thousand.

Lost Gip. Forty-sixth thousand.

The King's Servants. Thirty-third thousand.

Also a handsomely-bound Edition, with 12 Illustrations, price 2s. 6d.

PRICE SIXPENCE EACH.

With Frontispiece, Small Square, Limp Cloth.

Friends till Death.	**Two Christmas Stories.**
Old Transome.	**Michel Lorio's Cross.**

The Worth of a Baby, and How Apple Tree Court was Won.

POETRY.

ALLADS OF GOOD DEEDS, AND OTHER
Verses. By HENRY ABBEY. Foolscap 8vo, cloth, gilt,
price 5s.

Lyrics of Love, from Shakespeare to Tennyson. Selected
and arranged by W. DAVENPORT ADAMS, Jun. Foolscap 8vo, cloth
extra, gilt edges, price 3s. 6d.

Through Storm and Sunshine. By ADON. Illustrated by
M. E. Edwards, A. T. H. Paterson, and the Author. Crown 8vo.,
cloth, price 7s. 6d.

Pindar in English Rhyme. Being an attempt to render the
Epinikian Odes with the principal remaining Fragments of Pindar, into
English Rhymed Verse. By T. C. BARING, M.P., late Fellow of
Brasenose College, Oxford. Small quarto, cloth, price 7s.

Home Songs for Quiet Hours. By the Rev. Canon
R. H. BAYNES, Editor of "Lyra Anglicana," &c. Second Edition.
Foolscap 8vo, cloth extra, price 3s. 6d.

This may also be had handsomely bound in Morocco with gilt edges.

Metrical Translations from the Greek and Latin Poets,
and other Poems. By R. B. BOSWELL, M.A., Oxon. Crown 8vo
cloth, price 5s.

Poems. By WILLIAM CULLEN BRYANT. Red-line Edition,
With 24 Illustrations and Portrait of the Author. Square Crown 8vo,
cloth, price 7s. 6d.

A Cheaper Edition, with Frontispiece, cloth, price 3s. 6d.

Poems by Dr. W. C. BENNETT.

Songs for Sailors. Dedicated by Special Request to H.R.H. the Duke of Edinburgh. With Steel Portrait and Illustrations. Crown 8vo, cloth, price 3s. 6d.

An Edition in Illustrated Paper Covers, price 1s.

Baby May. Home Poems and Ballads. With Frontispiece. Cloth elegant, Crown 8vo, cloth, price 6s.

Baby May and Home Poems. Foolscap 8vo, sewed in Coloured Wrapper. Price 1s.

Narrative Poems and Ballads. Foolscap 8vo, sewed in Coloured Wrapper. Price 1s.

Poems by ROBERT BUCHANAN.

Poetical Works. Collected Edition, in 3 Vols., price 6s. each.
Vol. I.—" Ballads and Romances ;" " Ballads and Poems of Life ;" and a Portrait of the Author.
Vol. II.—" Ballads and Poems of Life ;" " Allegories and Sonnets."
Vol. III.—"Cruiskeen Sonnets;" "Book of Orm;" "Political Mystics."

Walled in, and Other Poems. By the Rev. HENRY J. BULKELEY. Crown 8vo, cloth, price 5s.

Calderon's Dramas: The Wonder-Working Magician—Life is a Dream—The Purgatory of St. Patrick. Translated by Denis Florence McCarthy. Post 8vo, cloth, price 10s.

Narcissus and Other Poems. By E. CARPENTER. Fcap. 8vo, cloth, price 5s.

Pretty Lessons in Verse for Good Children, with some Lessons in Latin, in Easy Rhyme. By SARA COLERIDGE. A New Edition. Illustrated. Foolscap 8vo, cloth, price 3s. 6d.

Cosmos. A Poem. Foolscap 8vo, cloth, price 3s. 6d.
Subjects—Nature in the Past and in the Present—Man in the Past and in the Present—The Future.

Poems by AUBREY DE VERE.

Alexander the Great. A Dramatic Poem. Small crown 8vo, cloth, price 5s.

The Infant Bridal, and other Poems. A New and Enlarged Edition. Foolscap 8vo, cloth, price 7s. 6d.

The Legends of St. Patrick, and other Poems. Small Crown 8vo, cloth, price 5s.

English Sonnets. Collected and arranged by JOHN DENNIS. Foolscap 8vo, cloth, price 3s. 6d.

Vignettes in Rhyme and Vers de Societe. By AUSTIN DOBSON. Second Edition. Foolscap 8vo, cloth, price 5s.

Hymns and Verses. Original and Translated. By the Rev. HENRY DOWNTON, M.A. Small Crown 8vo, cloth, price 3s. 6d.

Minor Chords; or, Songs for the Suffering: A Volume of Verse. By the Rev. BASIL EDWARDS. Foolscap 8vo, cloth, price 3s. 6d.; paper, price 2s. 6d.

The Epic of Hades. By a New Writer. Author of "Songs of Two Worlds." Foolscap 8vo, cloth, price 5s.

Eros Agonistes. Poems. By E.B.D. Foolscap 8vo, cloth, price 3s. 6d.

Hymns for the Church and Home. Selected and Edited by the Rev. W. FLEMING STEVENSON.

The Hymn Book consists of Three Parts:—I. For Public Worship.—II. For Family and Private Worship.—III. For Children.

Published in various forms and prices, the latter ranging from 8d. to 6s. Lists and full particulars will be furnished on application to the Publishers.

On Viol and Flute. By EDMUND W. GOSSE. With Title-page specially designed by William B. Scott. Crown 8vo, cloth, price 5s.

A Tale of the Sea, Sonnets, and other Poems. By JAMES HOWELL. Foolscap 8vo, cloth, price 5s.

MR. TENNYSON'S WORKS.

Queen Mary: a Drama. New Edition, price 6s.

Mr. Tennyson's Works. The Author's Edition.

    Vol. I.—Early Poems and English Idylls, cloth, price 6s.; Rox., 7s. 6d.
        II.—Locksley Hall, Lucretius, & other Poems ,, 6s. ,, 7s. 6d.
        III.—The Idylls of the King, complete   ,, 7s. 6d. ,, 9s.
        IV.—The Princess and Maud   ,, 6s. ,, 7s. 6d.
        V.—Enoch Arden and In Memoriam   ,, 6s. ,, 7s. 6d.
    Price 31s. 6d. cloth gilt, or 39s. half-morocco, Roxburgh style.

Mr. Tennyson's Works. The Cabinet Edition. In 10 Half-Crown Volumes, each with a Frontispiece. These Volumes may be had separately, or the Edition complete, in handsome ornamental case, price 28s.

CONTENTS.

    Vol. I.—Early Poems. Illustrated with a Photographic Portrait of Mr. Alfred Tennyson.
        II.—English Idylls, and other Poems. Containing an Engraving of Mr. Alfred Tennyson's Residence at Aldworth.
        III.—Locksley Hall, and other Poems. With an Engraved Picture of Farringford.
        IV.—Lucretius, and other Poems. Containing an Engraving of a Scene in the Garden at Swainston.
        V.—Idylls of the King. With an Autotype of the Bust of Mr. Alfred Tennyson, by T. Woolner, R.A.
        VI.—Idylls of the King. Illustrated, with an Engraved Portrait of "Elaine," from a Photographic Study by Julia M. Cameron.
        VII.—Idylls of the King. Containing an Engraving of "Arthur," from a Photographic Study by Julia M. Cameron.
        VIII.—The Princess. With an Engraved Frontispiece.
        IX.—Maud and Enoch Arden. With a Picture of "Maud," taken from a Photographic Study by Julia M. Cameron.
        X.—In Memoriam. With a Steel Engraving of Arthur H. Hallam, Engraved from a Picture in possession of the Author by J. C. Armitage.

Mr. Tennyson's Works. The Library Edition. This Edition is in 6 octavo Volumes, printed in large, clear old-faced type, with a Steel Engraved Portrait of the Author, each volume price 10s. 6d., or the set complete, £3 3s.

CONTENTS.

Vol. I.—Miscellaneous Poems.
II.—Miscellaneous Poems.
III.—Princess and other Poems.
IV.—In Memoriam and Maud.
V.—Idylls of the King.
VI.—Idylls of the King.

Mr. Tennyson's Works. The Miniature Edition. In 11 Volumes, pocket size, bound in imitation vellum, ornamented in gilt and gilt edges, in case, price 35s. This Edition can also be had in plain binding and case, price 31s. 6d.; gilt extra, 35s.

Mr. Tennyson's Works. The Original Editions. Green cloth lettered.

		s.	d.
Poems ... ... reduced from 9s. to		6	0
Maud and other Poems ... ... ,, ,, 5s. ,,		3	6
The Princess ... ... ,, ,, 5s. ,,		3	6
Idylls of the King ... ... ,, ,, 7s. ,,		5	0
The Holy Grail ... ... ,, ,, 7s. ,,		4	6
Gareth and Lynette ... ... ,, ,, 5s. ,,		3	0
Idylls of the King, collected ... ... ,, ,, 12s. ,,		6	0
Enoch Arden ... ... ,, ,, 6s. ,,		3	6
In Memoriam ... ... ,, ,, 6s. ,,		4	0

All the various editions of Mr. Tennyson's Works may also be had in elegant binding, calf, Morocco, or Russia.

Selections from the Works of Mr. Tennyson. Cloth, reduced from 5s. to 3s. 6d., or gilt extra, 4s.

Songs from the Works of Mr. Tennyson. Reduced from 5s. to 3s. 6d., gilt extra, 4s.

Penelope, and Other Poems. By ALLISON HUGHES. Foolscap 8vo, cloth, price 4s. 6d.

Poems by Mrs. HAMILTON KING.

The Disciples. A New Poem. Second Edition, with some Notes. Crown 8vo, cloth, price 7s. 6d.

Aspromonte, and Other Poems. Second Edition. Foolscap 8vo, cloth, price 4s. 6d.

Poems. By ANNETTE F. C. KNIGHT. Foolscap 8vo, cloth, price 5s.

The Lady of Lipari. A Poem in Three Cantos. Foolscap 8vo, cloth, price 5s.

The Gallery of Pigeons, and other Poems. By THEOPHILE MARZIALS. Crown 8vo, cloth, price 4s. 6d.

The Olympian and Pythian Odes of Pindar. A New Translation in English Verse. By the Rev. F. D. MORICE, M.A., Fellow of Queen's College, Oxford. Crown 8vo, cloth, price 7s. 6d.

The Inner and Outer Life Poems. By the Rev. A. NORRIS, B.A. Foolscap 8vo, cloth, price 6s.

Göethe's Faust. A New Translation in Rime. By C. KEGAN PAUL. Crown 8vo, cloth, price 6s.

Timoleon. A Dramatic Poem. By JAMES RHOADES. Foolscap 8vo, cloth, price 5s.

The Dream and the Deed, and other Poems. By PATRICK SCOTT. Foolscap 8vo, cloth, price 5s.

Songs of Two Worlds. By a New Writer. First Series. Second Edition, Foolscap 8vo, cloth, price 5s.

Songs of Two Worlds. By a New Writer. Second Series. Second Edition, Foolscap 8vo, cloth, price 5s.

Songs of Two Worlds. By a New Writer. Third Series. Second Edition, Foolscap 8vo, cloth, price 5s.

Songs for Music. By Four Friends. Square crown 8vo, cloth, price 5s. Containing Songs by—

    Reginald A. Gatty. | Greville J. Chester.
    Stephen H. Gatty. | Juliana H. Ewing.

Monacella: a Legend of North Wales. A Poem. By AGNES STONEHEWER, Foolscap 8vo, cloth, price 3s. 6d.

Poems. By the Rev. J. W. AUGUSTUS TAYLOR, M.A. Foolscap 8vo, cloth, price 5s.

Poems by Sir HENRY TAYLOR.

Edwin the Fair and Isaac Comnenus. Foolscap 8vo, cloth, price 3s. 6d.

A Sicilian Summer and Other Poems. Foolscap 8vo, cloth, price 3s. 6d.

Philip Van Artevelde. A Dramatic Poem. Foolscap 8vo, cloth, price 5s.

Thoughts in Verse. Small crown 8vo, cloth, price 1s. 6d.

Hymns and Sacred Lyrics. By the Rev. GODFREY THRING, B.A. Foolscap 8vo, cloth, price 5s.

Arvan; or, the Story of the Sword. A Poem. By HERBERT TODD, M.A. Crown 8vo, cloth, price 7s. 6d.

Sonnets, Lyrics, and Translations. By the Rev. CHARLES TURNER. Crown 8vo, cloth, price 4s. 6d.

On the North Wind—Thistledown. A Volume of Poems. By the Hon. Mrs. WILLOUGHBY. Small Crown 8vo, cloth, price 7s. 6d.

FICTION.

The Cornhill Library of Fiction. Crown 8vo, cloth, price 3s. 6d. each.

HALF-A-DOZEN DAUGHTERS. By J. Masterman.

The House of Raby. By Mrs. G. Hooper.

A Fight for Life. By Moy Thomas.

Robin Gray. By Charles Gibbon.

Kitty. By Miss M. Betham-Edwards.

One of Two; or the Left-Handed Bride. By J. Hain Friswell.

Ready-Money Mortiboy. A Matter-of-Fact Story.

God's Providence House. By Mrs. G. L. Banks.

For Lack of Gold. By Charles Gibbon.

Hirell. By John Saunders.

Abel Drake's Wife. By John Saunders.

Culmshire Folk. A Novel. By IGNOTUS. New and Cheaper Edition in 1 vol. Crown 8vo, price 6s.

Her Title of Honour. A Book for Girls. By HOLME LEE. New Edition, with a Frontispiece, Crown 8vo, cloth, price 5s.

Russian Romance. By ALEXANDER SERGUEVITCH POUSHKIN. Translated from the Tales of Belkin, &c. By Mrs. J. Buchan Telfer (*née* Mouravieff). Crown 8vo, cloth, price 7s. 6d.

Memoirs of Mrs. Lætitia Boothby. By WILLIAM CLARK RUSSELL. Crown 8vo, price 7s. 6d.

Works by KATHERINE SAUNDERS. Crown 8vo, price 6s. each.

Gideon's Rock, and other Stories.

Joan Merryweather, and other Stories.

Margaret and Elizabeth. A Story of the Sea.

Works by Col. MEADOWS TAYLOR, C.S.I., M.R.I.H. Crown 8vo, cloth, price 6s. each.

The Confessions of a Thug.

Tara: a Mahratta Tale.

The Romantic Annals of a Naval Family. By Mrs. ARTHUR TRAHERNE. A New and Cheaper Edition, crown 8vo, cloth. price 5s.

HISTORY AND TRAVEL.

THE HISTORY OF JAPAN. From the Earliest Period to the Present Time. By F. O. ADAMS, H.B.M.'s Secretary of Embassy at Paris, formerly H.B.M.'s Chargé d'Affaires, and Secretary of Legation at Yedo. New Edition revised. In 2 vols., with Maps and Plans. Demy 8vo, cloth, price 21s. each

The Ashantee War. A Popular Narrative. By the Special Correspondent of the Daily News. Crown 8vo, cloth, price 6s.

The Russians in Central Asia. A Critical Examination, down to the present time, of the Geography and History of Central Asia. By Baron F. VON HELLWALD. Translated by Lieut.-Col. Theodore Wirgman, LL.B. With Map. Large Post 8vo, cloth, price 12s.

Western India before and during the Mutinies. Pictures drawn from life. By Maj.-Gen. G. LE GRAND JACOB, K.C.S.I., C.B. Second Edition, Crown 8vo, cloth, price 7s. 6d.

The Norman People, and their Existing Descendants in the British Dominions and the United States of America. Demy 8vo, cloth, price 21s.

Echoes of a Famous Year. By HARRIETT PARR. Crown 8vo, cloth, price 8s. 6d.

Persia—Ancient and Modern. By JOHN PIGGOTT, F.S.A., F.R.G.S., Post 8vo, cloth, price 10s. 6d.

Works by NASSAU WILLIAM SENIOR.

Alexis De Tocqueville. Correspondence and Conversation with Nassau W. Senior, from 1833 to 1859. Edited by M.C.M. Simpson. 2 vols. Large Post 8vo, cloth, price 21s.

Journals kept in France and Italy. From 1848 to 1852. With a Sketch of the Revolution of 1848. Edited by his daughter, M. C. M. Simpson. 2 vols, Post 8vo, cloth, price 24s.

History of the English Revolution of 1688. By C. D. YONGE, Regius Professor, Queen's College, Belfast. Crown 8vo, cloth, price 6s.

Rough Notes of a Visit to Belgium, Sedan, and Paris. in September, 1870-71. By JOHN ASHTON. Crown 8vo, cloth, price 3s. 6d.

Field and Forest Rambles of a Naturalist in New Brunswick. With Notes and Observations on the Natural History of Eastern Canada. By A. L. ADAMS, M.A. Illustrated, 8vo, cloth, price 14s.

Eastern Experiences. Illustrated with Maps and Diagrams. By L. BOWRING, C.S.I., Lord Canning's Private Secretary, and for many years Chief Commissioner of Mysore and Coorg. Demy 8vo, cloth, price 16s.

The Inner Life of Syria, Palestine, and the Holy Land. By Mrs. RICHARD BURTON. Second Edition. 2 vols, Demy 8vo, cloth, price 24s.

Round the World in 1870. A Volume of Travels, with Maps. By A. D. CARLISLE, B.A., Trin. Coll., Camb. New and Cheaper Edition. Demy 8vo, cloth, price 6s.

Missionary Enterprise in the East. With special reference to the Syrian Christians of Malabar, and the results of modern Missions. With Four Illustrations. By the Rev. RICHARD COLLINS, M.A. Crown 8vo, cloth, price 6s.

Mountain, Meadow, and Mere. A Series of Outdoor Sketches of Sport, Scenery, Adventures, and Natural History. With Sixteen Illustrations by Bosworth W. Harcourt. By G. CHRISTOPHER DAVIES. Crown 8vo, cloth, price 6s.

The Nile without a Dragoman. By FREDERIC EDEN. Second Edition, Crown 8vo, cloth, price 7s. 6d.

Missionary Life in the Southern Seas. By JAMES HUTTON. With Illustrations. Crown 8vo, cloth, price 7s. 6d.

Letters from China and Japan. By L. D. S. With Illustrated Title-page, Crown 8vo, cloth, price 7s. 6d.

The Truth about Ireland. A Tour of Observation, with Remarks on Irish Public Questions. By JAMES MACAULAY, M.A., M.D., Edin. A New and Cheaper Edition. Crown 8vo, cloth, price 3s. 6d.

Wayside Notes in Scandinavia. Being Notes of Travel in the North of Europe. By MARK ANTONY LOWER, M.A., F.S.A. Crown 8vo, cloth, price 9s.

The Alps of Arabia; or, Travels through Egypt, Sinai, Arabia, and the Holy Land. By WILLIAM CHARLES MAUGHAN. With Map. A New and Cheaper Edition. Demy 8vo, cloth, price 5s.

An Autumn Tour in the United States and Canada. By Lieut.-Col. J. G. MEDLEY, Royal Engineers. Crown 8vo, cloth, price 5s.

A Winter in Morocco. With 4 Illustrations. By AMELIA PERRIER. A New and Cheaper Edition, Crown 8vo, cloth, price 3s. 6d.

Spitzbergen—the Gateway to the Polynia; or, A Voyage to Spitzbergen. With numerous Illustrations by Whymper and others, and Map. By Captain JOHN C. WELLS, R.N. New and Cheaper Edition, 8vo, cloth, price 6s.

The Mishmee Hills: an Account of a Journey made in an Attempt to Penetrate Thibet from Assam, to open New Routes for Commerce. By T. T. COOPER. Second Edition. With Four Illustrations and Map. Demy 8vo, cloth, price 10s. 6d.

'Ilam En Nas. Historical Tales and Anecdotes of the Times of the Early Khalifahs. Translated from the Arabic Originals. Illustrated with Historical and Explanatory Notes. By Mrs. GODFREY CLERK, Author of "The Antipodes and Round the World." Crown 8vo, cloth, price 7s.

Tent Life with English Gipsies in Norway. With Five full-page Engravings and Thirty-one smaller Illustrations by Whymper and others, and Map of the Country showing Routes. By HUBERT SMITH. Third Edition. Revised and Corrected. 8vo, price 21s.

BIOGRAPHY.

JOHN GREY (of Dilston); MEMOIRS. By his Daughter, JOSEPHINE E. BUTLER. New and Cheaper Edition. Crown 8vo, cloth, price 3s. 6d.

The Life of Samuel Lover, R.H.A.; Artistic, Literary, and Musical. With Selections from his Unpublished Papers and Correspondence. By BAYLE BERNARD. 2 Vols. With a Portrait. Post 8vo, cloth, price 21s.

The Earls of Middleton, Lords of Clermont and of Fettercairn, and the Middleton Family. By A. C. BISCOE. Crown 8vo, cloth, price 10s. 6d.

Leonora Christina, Memoirs of, Daughter of Christian IV. of Denmark; Written during her Imprisonment in the Blue Tower of the Royal Palace at Copenhagen, 1663-1685. Translated by F. E. Bunnètt. With an Autotype Portrait of the Princess. A New and Cheaper Edition. Medium 8vo, cloth, price 5s.

Memoir and Letters of Sara Coleridge. Edited by her Daughter. Third Edition, Revised and Corrected. With Index. 2 vols. With 2 Portraits. Crown 8vo, cloth, price 24s.
Cheap Edition. With one Portrait. Crown 8vo, cloth, price 7s. 6d.

Joseph Mazzini: a Memoir. By E. A. V. With two Essays by Mazzini—"Thoughts on Democracy," and "The Duties of Man." Dedicated to the Working Classes by P. H. Taylor, M.P. With Two Portraits. Crown 8vo, cloth, price 3s. 6d.

Mrs. Gilbert, formerly Ann Taylor, Autobiography and other Memorials of. Edited by Josiah Gilbert. New and Revised Edition. In 2 vols. With 2 Steel Portraits and several Wood Engravings. Post 8vo, cloth, price 24s.

The Vicar of Morwenstow: a Memoir of the Rev. R. S. HAWKER. By the Rev. S. BARING-GOULD. New and Revised edition. With Portrait. Post 8vo, cloth, price 10s. 6d.

Autobiography of A. B. Granville, F.R.S., &c. Edited, with a brief account of the concluding years of his life, by his youngest Daughter, PAULINA B. GRANVILLE. 2 vols. With a Portrait. Demy 8vo, cloth, price 32s.

William Augustus, Duke of Cumberland: Being a Sketch of his Military Life and Character, chiefly as exhibited in the General Orders of his Royal Highness, 1745—1747. By ARCHIBALD NEIL CAMPBELL MACLACHLAN, M.A. With Illustrations. Post 8vo, cloth, price 15s.

Characteristics from the Writings of Dr. J. H. Newman. Being Selections, Personal, Historical, Philosophical, and Religious, from his various Works. Arranged with the Author's personal approval. Second Edition. With Portrait. Crown 8vo, cloth, price 6s.

William Godwin: his Friends and Contemporaries. With Portraits and Facsimiles of the handwriting of Godwin and his Wife. By C. KEGAN PAUL. 2 vols. Demy 8vo, cloth, price 28s.

The late Rev. F. W. Robertson, M.A., Life and Letters of. Edited by STOPFORD BROOKE, M.A.
I. In 2 vols., uniform with the Sermons. Steel Portrait. 7s. 6d.
II. Library Edition. 8vo. Two Steel Portraits. 12s.
III. A Popular Edition, in 1 vol. 8vo. 6s.

Life and Letters of Rowland Williams, D.D. With Selections from his Note-books. Edited by Mrs. ROWLAND WILLIAMS. With a Photographic Portrait. 2 vols. Large post 8vo, cloth, price 24s.

Shelley Memorials from Authentic Sources. With (now first printed) an Essay on Christianity by PERCY BYSSHE SHELLEY. With Portrait. Third Edition. Crown 8vo, cloth, price 5s.

Memoirs of Gen. W. T. Sherman, Commander of the Federal Forces in the American Civil War. By Himself. With Map. 2 vols. Demy 8vo, cloth, price 24s. *Copyright English Edition.*

Cabinet Portraits. Biographical Sketches of Statesmen of the Day. By T. WEMYSS REID. Crown 8vo, cloth, price 7s. 6d.

THEOLOGY.

 **SCOTCH COMMUNION SUNDAY**, to which are added Certain Discourses from a University City. By A. K. H. B., the Author of "The Recreations of a Country Parson. Second Edition. Crown 8vo, cloth, price 5s.

Abraham : his Life, Times, and Travels, as told by a Contemporary 3,800 years ago. With Map. By the Rev. R. ALLEN, M.A. Post 8vo, cloth, price 10s. 6d.

Works by the Rev. CHARLES ANDERSON, M.A.

Church Thought and Church Work. Edited by. Second Edition, Demy 8vo, cloth, price 7s. 6d.

Containing Articles by the Revs.—

J. M. Capes,
Professor Cheetham,
J. Ll. Davis,
Harry Jones,

Brooke Lambert,
A. J. Ross,
The Editor,
And others.

Words and Works in a London Parish. Edited by. Second Edition, Demy 8vo, cloth, price 6s.

The Curate of Shyre. Second Edition. 8vo, cloth, price 7s. 6d.

New Readings of Old Parables. Demy 8vo, cloth, price 4s. 6d.

The Eternal Life. Sermons by the Rev. JAS. NOBLE BENNIE, M.A. Crown 8vo, cloth, price 6s.

Works by the Rev. J. BALDWIN BROWN, B.A.

The Higher Life. Its Reality, Experience, and Destiny. Fourth Edition, Crown 8vo, cloth, price 7s. 6d.

The Doctrine of Annihilation in the Light of the Gospel of Love. Five Discourses. Second Edition Crown 8vo, cloth, price 2s. 6d.

Until the Day Dawn. Four Advent Lectures By the Rev. MARMADUKE E. BROWNE. Crown 8vo, cloth, price 2s. 6d.

Works by W. G. BROOKE, M.A., Barrister-at-Law.

The Public Worship Regulation Act. With a Classified Statement of its Provisions, Notes, and Index. Third Edition, revised and corrected, Crown 8vo, cloth, price 3s. 6d.

Six Privy Council Judgments—1850-1872. Annotated by. Third Edition, Crown 8vo, cloth, price 9s.

Works by the Rev. STOPFORD A. BROOKE, M.A.,
Chaplain-in-Ordinary to H.M. the Queen.

Theology in the English Poets. Cowper, Coleridge, Wordsworth, and Burns. Second Edition, post 8vo, cloth, price 9s.

Freedom in the Church of England. Six Sermons suggested by the Voysey judgment. Second Edition, Crown 8vo, cloth, price 3s. 6d.

Christ in Modern Life. Sermons. Eighth Edition, Crown 8vo, cloth, price 7s. 6d.

Sermons. First Series, Eighth Edition, Crown 8vo, cloth. price 6s.

Sermons. Second Series, Third Edition, Crown 8vo, cloth, price 7s.

The Life and Work of Frederick Denison Maurice. A Memorial Sermon. Crown 8vo, sewed, price 1s.

The Realm of Truth. By Miss E. T. CARNE. Crown 8vo, cloth, price 5s. 6d.

The New Testament, translated from the latest Greek Text of Tischendorf. By SAMUEL DAVIDSON, D.D., LL.D. A new and thoroughly revised Edition. Post 8vo, cloth, price 10s. 6d.

Why am I a Christian? By Viscount STRATFORD DE REDCLIFFE, P.C., K.G., G.C.B. Fifth Edition, Crown 8vo, cloth, price 3s.

Works by the Rev. G. S. DREW, M.A., Vicar of Trinity, Lambeth.

The Son of Man, His Life and Ministry. Crown 8vo, cloth, price 7s. 6d.

Scripture Lands in Connection with their History. Second Edition, 8vo, cloth, price 10s. 6d.

Nazareth : Its Life and Lessons. Third Edition, Crown 8vo, cloth, price 5s.

The Divine Kingdom on Earth as it is in Heaven. Demy 8vo, cloth, price 10s. 6d.

An Essay on the Rule of Faith and Creed of Athanasius. By an ENGLISH CLERGYMAN. 8vo, sewed, price 1s.

A Book of Common Prayer and Worship for House-hold use, compiled from the Holy Scriptures. By MARK EVANS. Foolscap 8vo, cloth, price 2s. 6d.

Studies of the Divine Master. By the Rev. T. GRIFFITH, A.M., Prebendary of St. Paul's. Demy 8vo, cloth, price 12s.

Rugby School Sermons. By HENRY HAYMAN, D.D., late Head Master of Rugby School. With an Introductory Essay on the Indwelling of the Holy Spirit. Crown 8vo, cloth, price 7s. 6d.

Works by the Rev. H. R. HAWEIS, M.A.

Speech in Season. Third Edition. Crown 8vo, cloth, price 9s.

Thoughts for the Times. Ninth Edition. Crown 8vo, cloth, price 7s. 6d.

Unsectarian Family Prayers, for Morning and Evening for a Week, with short selected passages from the Bible. Square Crown 8vo cloth, price 3s. 6d.

The Privilege of Peter, Legally and Historically Examined, and the claims of the Roman Church compared with the Scriptures, the Councils, and the Testimony of the Popes themselves. By the Rev. R. C. JENKINS, M.A., Rector of Lyminge, and Honorary Canon of Canterbury. Foolscap 8vo, cloth, price 3s. 6d.

The Gospel its own Witness. By the Rev. STANLEY LEATHES. Crown 8vo, cloth, price 5s.

John Knox and the Church of England : His Work in her Pulpit and his Influence upon her Liturgy, Articles, and Parties. By PETER LORIMER, D.D. Demy 8vo, cloth, price 12s.

Essays on Religion and Literature. By various Writers. Edited by His Eminence Cardinal MANNING. Demy 8vo, cloth, price 10s. 6d.

CONTENTS.

The Philosophy of Christianity.
Mystic Elements of Religion.
Controversy with the Agnostics.
A Reasoning Thought.
Darwinism brought to Book.

Mr. Mill on Liberty of the Press
Christianity in relation to Society.
The Religious Condition of Germany.
The Philosophy of Bacon.

Catholic Laymen and Scholastic Philosophy.

Sermonettes : on Synonymous Texts, taken from the Bible and Book of Common Prayer, for the Study, Family Reading, and Private Devotion. By the Rev. THOMAS MOORE, Vicar of Christ Church, Chesham. Small Crown 8vo, cloth, price 4s. 6d.

Christ and His Church. A Course of Lent Lectures, By the Rev. DANIEL MOORE, M.A., Author of "The Age and the Gospel," &c. Crown 8vo, cloth, price 3s. 6d.

The Paraclete : An Essay on the Personality and Ministry of the Holy Ghost, with some reference to current discussions. By JOSEPH PARKER, D.D. Second Edition. Demy 8vo, cloth, price 12s.

Unfoldings of Christian Hope : An Essay showing that the Doctrine contained in the Damnatory Clauses of the Creed commonly called Athanasian is unscriptural. By PRESBYTER. Small Crown 8vo, cloth, price 4s. 6d.

Works by the late Rev. F. W. ROBERTSON, M.A.

Sermons. New and Cheaper Editions.
    First Series.—Small Crown 8vo, cloth, price 3s. 6d.
    Second Series.—Small Crown 8vo, cloth, price 3s. 6d.
    Third Series.—Small Crown 8vo, cloth, price 3s. 6d.
    Fourth Series.—Small Crown 8vo, cloth, price 3s. 6d.

Expository Lectures on St. Paul's Epistle to the Corinthians. Small Crown 8vo, cloth, price 5s.

Lectures and Addresses, with other Literary Remains. A New Edition. Crown 8vo, cloth, price 5s.
    The above Works can also be had bound in half Morocco.

An Analysis of Mr. Tennyson's "In Memoriam." Dedicated, by Permission, to the Poet-Laureate. Foolscap 8vo, cloth, price 2s.

The Education of the Human Race. Translated from the German of Gotthold Ephraim Lessing. Foolscap 8vo, cloth, price 2s. 6d.

Studies in Modern Problems. By various Writers. Edited by the Rev. ORBY SHIPLEY, M.A. 2 vols. Crown 8vo, cloth, price 5s. each.

Home Words for Wanderers. A Volume of Sermons. By the Rev. A. S. THOMPSON, British Chaplain at St. Petersburg, Crown 8vo, cloth, price 6s.

Every Day a Portion. Adapted from the Bible and the Prayer Book, for the Private Devotions of those living in Widowhood. Collected and Edited by Lady MARY VYNER. Square Crown 8vo, cloth, price 5s.

WORKS by the Rev. C. J. VAUGHAN, D.D.

Words of Hope from the Pulpit of the Temple Church.
Third Edition. Crown 8vo, cloth, price 5s.

The Solidity of True Religion, and other Sermons.
Crown 8vo, cloth, price 3s. 6d.

Forget Thine Own People. An Appeal for Missions.
Crown 8vo, cloth, price 3s. 6d.

The Young Life Equipping Itself for God's Service.
Being Four Sermons Preached before the University of Cambridge, in November, 1872. Fourth Edition. Crown 8vo, cloth, price 3s. 6d.

Catholicism and the Vatican. With a Narrative of the Old Catholic Congress at Munich. By J. LOWRY WHITTLE, A.M., Trin. Coll., Dublin. Second Edition. Crown 8vo, cloth, price 4s. 6d.

The Church and the Empires. Historical Periods. By HENRY W. WILBERFORCE. Preceded by a Memoir of the Author by John Henry Newman, D.D., of the Oratory. With Portrait. Post 8vo, cloth, price 10s. 6d.

Works by the Rev. D. WRIGHT, of Stoke Bishop, Bristol.

Man and Animals. A Sermon. Crown 8vo, stitched in wrapper, price 1s.

Waiting for the Light, and other Sermons. Crown 8vo, cloth, price 6s.

SCIENCE.

HE PRINCIPLES of MENTAL PHYSIOLOGY.
By W. B. CARPENTER, LL.D., M.D., F.R.S., &c. Illustrated. Large post 8vo, cloth, price 12s.

The Scientific Societies of London. By BERNARD H. BECKER. Crown 8vo, cloth, price 5s.

Works by JAMES HINTON, late Aural Surgeon to Guy's Hospital.

The Place of the Physician. Being the Introductory Lecture at Guy's Hospital, 1873-74. To which is added Essays on the Law of Human Life, and on the Relation between Organic and Inorganic Worlds. Second Edition. Crown 8vo, cloth, price 3s. 6d.

Physiology for Practical Use. By various Writers. Second Edition. Illustrated. 2 vols., Crown 8vo, cloth, price 12s. 6d.

An Atlas of Diseases of the Membrana Tympani. With Descriptive Text. Post 8vo, price £6 6s.

The Questions of Aural Surgery. Illustrated. 2 vols., Post 8vo, cloth, price 12s. 6d.

Works by RICHARD A. PROCTOR.

Our Place among Infinities. A Series of Essays contrasting our little abode in space and time with the Infinities around us. To which are added Essays on "Astrology," and "The Jewish Sabbath." Second Edition. Crown 8vo, cloth, price 6s.

The Expanse of Heaven. A Series of Essays on the Wonders of the Firmament. With a Frontispiece. Second Edition. Crown 8vo, cloth, price 6s.

Works by Professor TH. RIBOT.

Contemporary English Psychology. Second Edition. Revised. Large post 8vo, cloth, price 9s.

Heredity: A Psychological Study on its Phenomena, its Laws, its Causes, and its Consequences. Large Crown 8vo, cloth, price 9s.

The Physics and Philosophy of the Senses; or, The Mental and the Physical in their Mutual Relation. Illustrated. By R. S. WYLD, F.R.S.E. Demy 8vo, cloth, price 16s.

Sensation and Intuition. By JAMES SULLY. Demy 8vo, cloth, price 10s. 6d.

THE INTERNATIONAL SCIENTIFIC SERIES.

1. **The Forms of Water in Clouds and Rivers, Ice and** Glaciers. By J. TYNDALL, LL.D., F.R.S. With 14 Illustrations. Sixth Edition. Crown 8vo, cloth, price 5s.

2. **Physics and Politics; or, Thoughts on the Application** of the Principles of "Natural Selection" and "Inheritance" to Political Society. By WALTER BAGEHOT. Third Edition. Crown 8vo, cloth, price 4s.

3. **Foods.** By EDWARD SMITH, M.D., LL.B., F.R.S. Profusely Illustrated. Fourth Edition. Crown 8vo, cloth, price 5s.

4. **Mind and Body: the Theories of their Relation.** By ALEXANDER BAIN, LL.D. With 4 Illustrations. Fifth Edition. Crown 8vo, cloth, price 4s.

5. **The Study of Sociology.** By HERBERT SPENCER. Fifth Edition. Crown 8vo, cloth, price 5s.

6. **On the Conservation of Energy.** By BALFOUR STEWART, M.D., LL.D., F.R.S. With 14 Engravings. Third Edition. Crown 8vo, cloth, price 5s.

7. **Animal Locomotion; or, Walking, Swimming, and** Flying. By J. B. PETTIGREW, M.D., F.R.S. With 119 Illustrations. Second Edition. Crown 8vo, cloth, price 5s.

8. **Responsibility in Mental Disease.** By H. MAUDSLEY, M.D. Second Edition. Crown 8vo, cloth, price 5s.

9. **The New Chemistry.** By Professor J. P. COOKE, of the Harvard University. With 31 Illustrations. Third Edition. Crown 8vo, cloth, price 5s.

10. **The Science of Law.** By Professor SHELDON AMOS. Second Edition. Crown 8vo, cloth, price 5s.

11. **Animal Mechanism.** A Treatise on Terrestrial and Aërial Locomotion. By Professor E. J. MAREY. With 117 Illustrations. Second Edition. Crown 8vo, cloth, price 5s.

12. **The Doctrine of Descent and Darwinism.** By Professor OSCAR SCHMIDT (Strasburg University). With 26 Illustrations. Third Edition. Crown 8vo, cloth, price 5s.

13. **The History of the Conflict between Religion and Science.** By Professor J. W. DRAPER. Seventh Edition. Crown 8vo, cloth, price 5s.

14. **Fungi: their Nature, Influences, Uses, &c.** By M. C. COOKE, M.A., LL.D. Edited by the Rev. M. J. Berkeley, M.A., F.L.S. With numerous Illustrations. Second Edition. Crown 8vo, cloth, price 5s.

15. **The Chemical Effects of Light and Photography.** By Dr. HERMANN VOGEL (Polytechnic Academy of Berlin). Translation thoroughly revised. With 100 Illustrations. Third Edition. Crown 8vo, cloth, price 5s.

16. **The Life and Growth of Language.** By WILLIAM DWIGHT WHITNEY, Professor of Sanskrit and Comparative Philology in Yale College, New Haven. Second Edition. Crown 8vo, cloth, price 5s.

17. **Money and the Mechanism of Exchange.** By Professor W. STANLEY JEVONS. Second Edition. Crown 8vo, cloth, price 5s.

18. **The Nature of Light: With a General Account of Physical Optics.** By Dr. EUGENE LOMMEL, Professor of Physics in the University of Erlangen. With 188 Illustrations, and a Table of Spectra in Chromolithography. Second Edition. Crown 8vo, cloth, price 5s.

19. **Animal Parasites & Messmates.** By M. VAN BENEDEN, Professor of the University of Louvain, Correspondent of the Institute of France. With 83 Illustrations. Second Edition. Crown 8vo, cloth, price 5s.

20. **Fermentation.** By Professor SCHUTZENBERGER, Director of the Chemical Laboratory at the Sorbonne. Second Edition. Crown 8vo, cloth, 5s.

21. **The Five Senses of Man.** By Professor BERNSTEIN, of the University of Halle. With 91 Illustrations. Crown 8vo, cloth, price 5s.

MISCELLANEOUS.

Works by WALTER BAGEHOT.

LOMBARD STREET. A Description of the Money Market. Sixth Edition. Crown 8vo, cloth, price 7s. 6d.

The English Constitution. A New Edition, Revised and corrected. Crown 8vo, cloth, price 7s. 6d.

Physics and Politics; or, Thoughts on the Application of the Principles of "Natural Selection" and "Inheritance" to Political Society. Third Edition. Crown 8vo, cloth, price 4s.

Volume II. of the International Scientific Series.

About My Father's Business. Work amidst the Sick, the Sad, and the Sorrowing. By THOMAS ARCHER. Crown 8vo, cloth, price 5s.

Studies in English. For the Use of Modern Schools. By H. C. Bowen, English Master Middle-Class City School, Cowper-street. Small Crown 8vo, cloth, price 1s. 6d.

Works by JOHN CROUMBIE BROWN, LL.D., &c.

Reboisement in France; or, Records of the Replanting of the Alps, the Cevennes, and the Pyrenees with Trees, Herbage, and Bush, with a view to arresting and preventing the destructive consequences and effects of Torrents. Demy 8vo, cloth, price 12s. 6d.

The Hydrology of Southern Africa. Demy 8vo, cloth, price 10s. 6d.

Republican Superstitions. Illustrated by the Political History of the United States. Including a correspondence with M. Louis Blanc. By MONCURE D. CONWAY. Crown 8vo, cloth, price 5s.

Works by EDWARD CLODD, F.R.A.S.

The Childhood of the World : a Simple Account of Man in Early Times. New Edition. Crown 8vo, cloth, price 3s.
A Special Edition for Schools. Limp cloth, price 1s.

The Childhood of Religions. Including a Simple Account of the Birth and Growth of Myths and Legends. Crown 8vo, cloth, price 5s.

Shakspere : a Critical Study of his Mind and Art. By EDWARD DOWDEN, LL.D. Second Edition. Post 8vo, cloth, price 12s.

The Better Self. Essays for Home Life. By J. HAIN FRISWELL. Crown 8vo, cloth, price 6s.

CONTENTS.

Beginning at Home.	Domestic Economy.
The Girls at Home.	On Keeping People Down.
The Wife's Mother.	Likes and Dislikes.
Pride in the Family.	On Falling Out.
Discontent and Grumbling.	Peace.

Myths and Songs of the South Pacific. With a Preface by F. Max Müller, M.A., Professor of Comparative Philology at Oxford, By the Rev. W. W. GILL. Post 8vo, cloth, price 9s.

Memorials of Millbank, and Chapters in Prison History. By Captain ARTHUR GRIFFITHS. With Illustrations. 2 vol . Post 8vo, cloth, price 21s.

The Other World ; or, Glimpses of the Supernatural. Being Facts, Records, and Traditions, relating to Dreams, Omens, Miraculous Occurrences, Apparitions, Wraiths, Warnings, Second-sight, Necromancy, Witchcraft, &c. By Rev. FREDERICK GEORGE LEE, D.C.L. A New Edition. 2 vols., Crown 8vo, cloth, price 15s.

Currency and Banking. By Professor BONAMY PRICE, Professor of Political Economy at Oxford. Crown 8vo, cloth, price 6s.

PORTRAITS OF AUTHORS.

Steel Engravings, Large India Proofs, Suitable for framing price 2s. 6d. each.

Dr. W. C. Bennett.
Robert Buchanan.
Sara Coleridge (Ætat. 17).
Sara Coleridge (in after years).
Mrs. Ann Gilbert.
Samuel Lover.
John Henry Newman.
F. W. Robertson.
Percy B. Shelley.
Alfred Tennyson.
H. W. Wilberforce.

UNWIN BROTHERS, PRINTERS, LONDON AND CHILWORTH.

www.ingramcontent.com/pod-product-compliance
Lightning Source LLC
Chambersburg PA
CBHW032226230426
43666CB00033B/1615